The Christchurch and Bournemouth Union Workhouse

The Christchurch and Bournemouth Union Workhouse

Sue Newman

Published by Sue Newman

Copyright © 1994 by Sue Newman

First Edition

First published in 1994 by Sue Newman, Fairhurst, 2 Magdalen Lane, Christchurch, Dorset BH23 1PH.

Tel: Christchurch 477686.

All rights reserved. No part of this work may be reproduced or stored in an information retrieval system (other than short extracts for the purposes of review) without the express permission of the publisher given in writing.

ISBN 0 9524856 0 5

Typeset, printed and bound by Bourne Press Limited, Bournemouth.

DEDICATION

Dedicated to the memory of **The Christchurch Times** *journalists, without whose meticulous and faithful reporting this record of the affairs of the Christchurch Workhouse would be immensely the poorer.*

Contents

Acknowledgements
Preface
Chapter One — the beginnings
Chapter Two — the early years
Chapter Three — later years
Chapter Four — workhouse life
Chapter Five — the end of the old workhouse
Chapter Six — the Red House
Chapter Seven — the new workhouse
Chapter Eight — the new regime
                 the workhouse children
                 the Cottage Homes
Chapter Nine — the public enquiry
Chapter Ten — the Edwardian era
Chapter Eleven — war
                 a hospital tribute
Chapter Twelve — on to the next war
                 memories of a Cottage Homes inmate
Chapter Thirteen — the NHS
                 last of the Cottage Homes
Postscript — later hospital history
Conclusion
Bibliography

Acknowledgements

I would like to thank the following for their contribution to this book, whether of information, photographs, advice or encouragement:
Mr Mike Allen, Mr Derek Beverley, Mr Gordon Bist, Miss Wendy Bowen, Miss Monica Brough-Slack, Miss Alison Carter, Miss Winifred Coffin, Mrs Grace Dargue, Mr Jack Dwyer, Mr Trevor Evans, Mrs Barbara Jones, Mr John Lewis, Mrs Charlotte Luckham, Mrs McGaw, Mrs Gladys Manton, Kathryn Morrison (Royal Commission on the Historical Monuments of England), Mrs Mabel Norman, Mr Joe Pilley, Mrs Violet Sawyer, Mr Ken Smith, Mr Ken Tullett and Mr H Weeks; also anyone else that I have inadvertently omitted from this list. One person I am very grateful to wished to remain anonymous.

I would also like to thank the following organisations which gave permission for material to be used in this book: *The Bournemouth Evening Echo*, The Bournemouth and Christchurch NHS Trust, *The Financial Times*, the Dorset Record Office, The Ordnance Survey Office and the Red House Museum.

Preface

100 YEARS' AGO

Sad death of Little Girl
Age 5½ years. Weight - 18lbs

On Tuesday morning an Inquest was held at the workhouse before Mr Bernard Hartfield, county coroner, touching the death of a little girl named Ethel Miller, aged 5 years, who died in that institution on Sunday last.

Mr A. E. Francis, solicitor, appeared to watch the proceedings on behalf of the local branch of the National Society for the Prevention of Cruelty to Children, and Police-Superintendant Haddon was also present. After the body had been viewed, the following evidence was adduced.

Inspector T. Hunt of the Bournemouth branch of the NSPCC stated that in consequence of some information he had received, he visited a cottage in Pound Lane, Christchurch, on the 27th March, accompanied by Police-Sargeant Hawkins. The mother of the deceased (Selina Miller) admitted him into the cottage, which was a four-roomed one. The deceased child was lying on a box, placed mouth upwards. There were nails driven into the sides and strings attached across from nail to nail. Over those was a small mattress, not quite the length of the box. On this the child was lying, covered up with a single sheet, one half of which was underneath the child's body. The mother said the father was upstairs, and he was called down. Witness asked the mother why she had allowed the child to be left in such a state, and she said, 'It's all right'. He (witness) said: 'Has any doctor seen it?' She said, 'Yes, Doctor Legate.' Asked when he first saw it, the mother said: 'The child was only taken ill seven weeks' ago, and at that time I sent for Dr Legate and he came once but did not come again for a month. At the end of the month I sent for him again.' Witness said: 'Why did you allow the child to remain here if you could not afford to keep it in a better condition, why did you not send it to the workhouse hospital?' She said: 'I don't want to do that.' Asked what she fed the child on, the mother replied: 'Doctor Legate is allowing me a pint of milk a day.'

The child appeared to be terribly emaciated and the surroundings as bad as it was possible to conceive. There was no fire in the place, no food that he could see, no furniture, the floor was damp and dirty, and the box in which the child was lying was placed immediately underneath the window. He (witness) questioned them as to their means, and the man said he could not earn very much. Witness's knowledge of his character was that it was not good; he could get drink very often. Witness told the parents that their want of means did not hinder them from placing the child where it would have comfort and attention. Witness asked whether there was no bed for the child to be upon and the woman said, 'Yes, but Doctor Legate says the child is not fit to be moved; it has to stay here day and night.' Witness went upstairs, but saw no bed at all. There was some cut straw upon the floor which had been used for sleeping on. The woman called his attention to some kind of tick that covered the straw, but she had taken it off to wash it. The man and wife admitted the child was theirs; they lived together but were not married. The child, though 5 years old, weighed only 19lbs. It ought to have weighed 40lbs at that age. Replying to the jurors, the inspector said the child did not speak to him. It lay quiet when he saw it, but when the mother moved it, it whined in a feeble manner. The body seemed a mere shell, and it lay crouched up with its knees almost close to its chin.

[Dr Legate testified that] in the interval before the 8th March, the mother had again been confined. There was no one to attend to her except an old woman, and very probably the child had not had its medicine regularly. When he (witness) saw the child the second time it was lying upon some kind of covering on the floor. The room was very uncleanly and offensive. He advised the mother to get the place tidy and provide a bed for the child to lie on. The next day she had the child in a large perambulator.

About 12 months ago they had another child die in the lodging-house. They now had four children with them, including the baby. The child was very dirty when admitted to the workhouse.

The Christchurch Times 1894.

The verdict was death caused by exhaustion following upon an abscess due to inflammation on the lungs. (The child, said Dr Legate, had had whooping cough followed by bronchial pneumonia.) There was a rider to the effect that the child's death was aggravated by the conditions of the surroundings.

This was Christchurch poverty in 1894.

It would probably have looked the same in 1794 or 1694.

CHAPTER ONE

the beginnings

It has often been said that the poor are always with us. This was as true in times long gone as it is today; the attempts made by the authorities in Christchurch to alleviate the distress of poverty before the advent of the modern welfare state form the subject matter of this book.

It would have been the vagaries of the weather and the effect on the farming cycle that would have accounted for most of the cases of poverty in the area, depending as it did until the latter part of the last century on agriculture and fishing. Other sources of income would have been cottage-based. Predominant amongst these was the knitting of stockings, which was common in Christchurch. At the end of the 18th century, approximately 1,000 of the poorer women in the area were engaged in this occupation (according to *The Hampshire Repository*, which also records an early Aldridge by the name of John, as one of the key employers). In addition to this there were other home-based industries - such as glove-making, spinning and, of course, those well-known local occupations, the legitimate fusee chain-making and the illicit smuggling of contraband.

No specific legislation existed until the 16th century, though the Priory Church certainly had a long and honourable record of assistance to the poor prior to the Dissolution, especially with gifts of food, and local charities were later set up with the same aim of alleviating distress (e.g. White's Charity, Elliott's, and, later, Coffin's charities).

Towards the end of the 16th century, the parish, like all others in the country, was obliged by law to appoint Overseers of the Poor, whose task, together with the churchwardens, was to find work for those without and construct a parish house for those unable to support themselves. These obligations were to be financed by the introduction of a Poor Rate levied on householders. Such poor persons that they were responsible for were only those from their own parishes; those from elsewhere were returned using force if necessary to what was known as their place of 'settlement'. This provision, further refined by the 1662 Act of Settlement, made lawyers rich in the ensuing centuries on the protracted squabbles between parishes anxious to avoid the expense of supporting a stranger, and was the cause of great social injustice; not the least of its effects being that those unable to find work in their home parish were unable to look elsewhere. Families could be split up, as legitimate children belonged to their parish of birth, whilst illegitimate ones belonged to the parish of their mother's birth, not necessarily the same thing. Widows could also be returned to their place of birth. Beggars who arrived from elsewhere were liable to be literally whipped out of the parish. All this would have made a person in dire need very wary of applying for parish relief. Although there did develop expedients by which a person could obtain settlement in another parish, such as obtaining employment for a year, it was never easy to attain, and in practice it was not uncommon for employers to sack the worker after 364 days in order not to create settlement rights for that person, which would have entitled them to parish relief.

It is against this general background that the building presently known as the Red House Museum came to be. The beginnings of this, the parish workhouse, have been documented in great detail by Herbert Druitt in *A Christchurch Miscellany*, written in 1924. He traces it back to a deed of 1745, when two acres of land in Quay Road, which was known, appropriately enough, as Monastery Street at this time, then occupied by a barn, skilling (shed or outhouse) and garden, was sold to the churchwardens and Overseers of the Poor of the parish. They had 'agreed

Red House Museum

to set or open a Workhouse for the more comfortable support of their numerous Poor'. It is not entirely clear what transpired in the intervening years, but the next deed documented is dated 1763 and describes the purchase of another 'messuage' and garden in the same street, by then known as Pitsdeep, in order to erect a workhouse. (A further confusing change of name for Quay Road is noted here: that in the latter part of the 19th century it was known as Mill Lane. Whitehall, its other road boundary, was known as Quomps Lane.) As soon as this was completed, a committee was formed from the overseers and churchwardens, together with 'Principal Inhabitants and Parishioners' (which august personages included well-known residents such as Charles Brander, Thomas Mews, Henry Mooring and Abraham Daw) to 'supervise the Purchasing building fiting up compleating furnishing Victualing and Governing' of the workhouse. This deed also records that 'the Poor of their said Parish were very numerous daily increasing and their maintenance very burthensome'. The reference to the increase in the numbers of those needing urgent relief is likely to have been a consequence of the enormous upheaval resulting from the Enclosure Acts of the time, which dispossessed the cottagers of their ancient rights to graze animals on common land. The workhouse was built soon after this date, probably in 1764.

This evidence is supported by references to the construction of a workhouse in the archives of the Overseers of the Poor. An entry in June 1763 announces that 'the principle intention of the Parishioners in erecting a workhouse is to restrain and prevent Idleness and Vice, to encourage industry and good manners, and to lesson (sic) the heavy charges occasioned by the present defective method of providing for their Poor. Now to prevent any doubt hereinafter as to the nature and original design of this useful undertaking, it is . . . declared and Agreed that the said workhouse to be erected for the Habitation of the Poor, is with an intent that they may be more decently and comfortably relieved and maintained; that none able to do any work may any longer be maintained in Idleness; but that the Poor, who shall inhabit the said House may be properly and constantly employed therein, according to their respective strength and abilities.'

Later, a reference is made in the accounts to a payment of 5s to Mr John Pardy for carrying turf to the workhouse (as fuel) 'to air it before the people went in'. These accounts were for the year ending April 1765, but the House seems to have taken in its first occupants in the preceding summer, as other entries indicate.

Vestry accounts of 1792 refer also to the purchase of a cottage 'in the gravel pits (the origin of the name 'Pitt's Deep'?). . . for the reception of such poor people of the . . . parish as shall not be thought proper to be received into the workhouse of the said parish'. Unfortunately, the records do not elaborate on the exact nature of the undesirable qualities of such people - whether they were vagrants, lunatics or unmarried mothers we can only speculate. It is also possible that such people may have been infectious, a situation addressed in 1806 by the conversion of a room 'at the north end of the Poor House into a hospital for the reception of such poor people within the Workhouse who may labour under diseases of a contagious or infecting nature . . . It is agreed and resolved that the same shall be forthwith done in the least expensive way that can be.' (Vestry Records.) Note the interchangeability of the terms 'poorhouse' and 'workhouse' at this time; it was about the middle of the 19th century before the latter term took precedence.

A few years' later, in 1814, the *Miscellany* records a further purchase of messuages at Pitt's Deep, which were thus added to the property.

The plan shows the ground floor layout. It dates from about 1870 (the 'Engine House' was the home of the parish fire engine) but this is how it may also have appeared in earlier times. The present entrance to the museum goes in to the men's ward, the hospital is now the site of the art gallery, the costume gallery occupies the schoolroom extension, and the women's wards have gone. The yards for men and boys are now a herb garden, and the girls' yard and drying green laid out with lawns and borders. A brick wall runs around the perimeter, very high on the Church Lane boundary, and a typical feature of workhouses in all areas. Such walls did not prevent all inmates from escaping, the most famous escapee from a workhouse being the great explorer, Sir Henry Stanley. Christchurch had its fair share of dissatisfied inmates who 'ran off' or 'absconded', according to the workhouse records.

Red House Museum as workhouse from O.S. 1870.

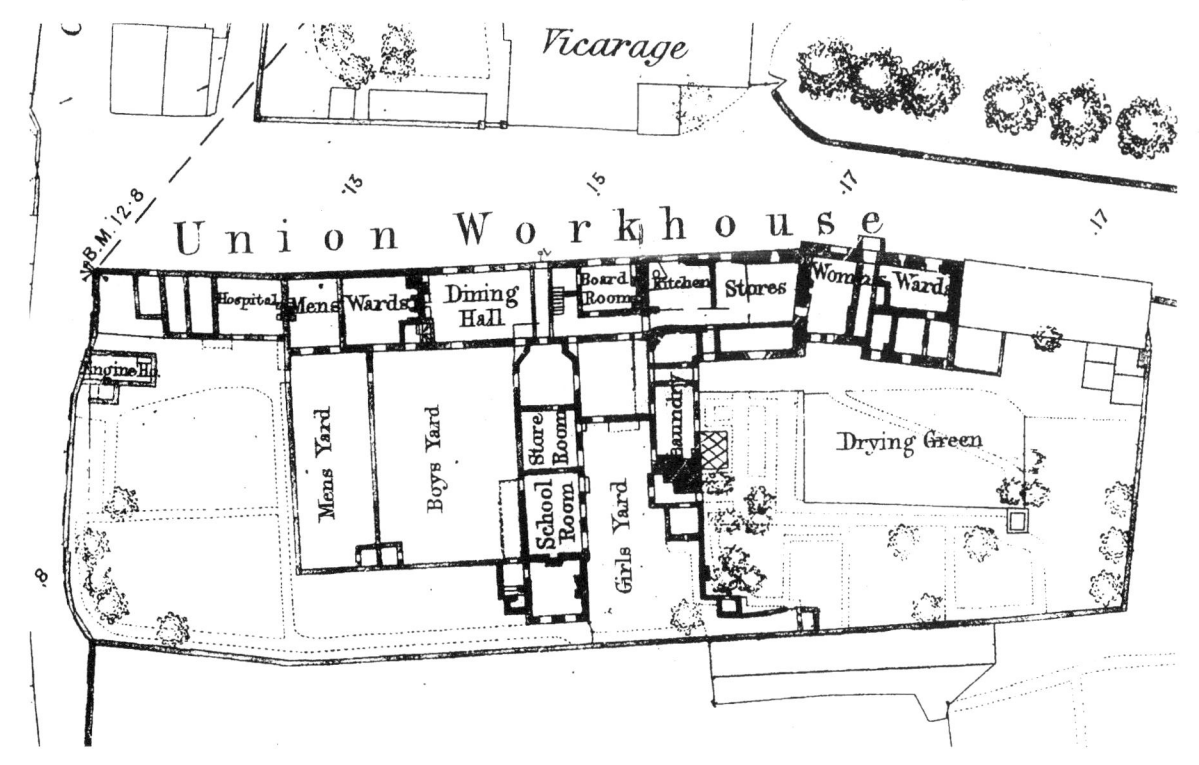

CHAPTER TWO

the early years

So who were the officials who were in charge of the workhouse; who were the inmates and what did they do?

To answer the first part of the question, it was the responsibility of the overseers and churchwardens to administer relief, whether 'out-relief' in the applicant's own home, or 'in the House'. The churchwardens at the time the workhouse was first built were John Cook, who was a well-known local brewer, and William Footner, of 'Muddiford'. The Overseers of the Poor were four in number and were: Edward Scott, Stephen Pack, George Verge and Thomas French. In 1824 the overseers were Messrs Hannaway, Best, Derham and Petty, and the churchwardens Messrs Spicer and Hopkins. It was not always possible to find people willing or able to undertake an overseer's functions; in 1811 James Penleaze (who built the original mansion at Highcliffe which preceded Highcliffe Castle) refused to take the office and was indicted for it. Others who took the position plainly did so to line their own pockets, the chief miscreant in this respect being one George Whiffen, who in 1856 was found to have expropriated the substantial sum, for those days, of £210. 10s 9d. He admitted having appropriated the Poor Rate funds and was convicted. He was duly despatched to the lock-up in Bargates (in Spicer Street in the Pit site, now demolished) whilst a distress warrant was issued against him in an attempt to recover some of the amount missing, but it was in vain, as he seems to have been possessed only of a couch and small bedstead to the value of £1 12s 6d. Mr Whiffen was sentenced to three months' imprisonment at Winchester's 'House of Correction'; to the regret of the magistrates this was the most severe sentence they could inflict.

The level of distress was widespread at the end of the 18th century, and for a short period it was the practice to top up the low wages of labourers with an allowance based on the prevailing price of bread. As the price of bread rose, they got an amount from the Poor Rate which was calculated in accordance with the size of their family and the price of a loaf (the Speenhamland system). This was much abused and very expensive. Examples of it being applied in Christchurch are taken from the Vestry Records, which record the overseers' decision that:

April 1795: 'By the unanimous wish, they are ready during the present high price of bread, to grant every reasonable relief to such poor parishioners as shall be found by enquiry to be peaceable, sober and industrious.'

December 1795: a proposal to increase the wages of labourers to 9s a week was approved, 'and that such increases of wages should continue during the present high price of bread and not be reduced until wheat shall be sold at 15s a load'.

Later, the overseers used their local knowledge of individuals and their circumstances or character to assist them with their decisions.

Thus, a Select Vestry account of their proceedings, in 1824, showed relief dispensed as follows:

sheets and blankets for a couple expecting a confinement - allowed;

a single man requesting money - allowed;

a petticoat requested - rejected; likewise requests for a shirt and a spade;

relief: wife ill - Dr Quartley ordered to attend;

a house - 'to look out for themselves';

several people were granted shoes, the commonest request;

a hedging hook - granted;

a window mended - rejected;

a bottle of port wine was granted to the parish surgeon (for medicinal purposes!);

relief - to go and see various named people, such applicants were ordered (it was the duty of ratepayers to provide work for relief applicants, an arrangement known as the 'roundsman' system).

One Harriet Tilley requested a spinning wheel. This was also a common request, as it was a means of enabling a widow, which Harriet may well have been, to earn a living without having to come into the House or require parish relief. In this case, the spinning wheel was allowed on condition that she 'returns her old one to this house and teaches no less than six children how to use it' - another means of keeping future applicants for relief at bay.

John Pardy asked for a house, but received only the peremptory response: 'To have only this house'. Others who applied for relief were offered only the House, not out-relief. A later (1824) case recorded one James Saunders 'ordered into the Poor House'. It may well have been that these last cases were able-bodied, a class of person always treated harshly by the authorities. It certainly demonstrates that the overseers selected, on what criteria is not recorded, who should get assistance and who should go without. The Rev. Bingley, writing in 1813, had only praise for their sagacity:

'The affairs of the poor are managed by a committee which meets every Monday morning at the workhouse. They hear the Complaints of the Poor, direct with what necessaries they are to be supplied, and on all occasions act with feeling and liberality. They purchase everything at first hand, and take care that whatever is purchased is good of the kind.'

The direct administration of the workhouse itself was in the hands of the Master, appointed by the vestry, and his wife, the Matron. At the time, there was no training for such posts, and the pay was poor, compared, for instance, to the prison service. The quality of recruit sometimes reflected this. The earliest Master recorded was one John Short in 1805, and his name crops up in the Vestry Minutes in connection with a riot. Not, as you might think, the inmates protesting about the conditions, but in connection with the Master. For 'repeated misconduct' (unfortunately, not detailed), he was dismissed, and, pending this taking effect, 'two proper men' were to be sworn in as special constables 'to prevent any disorder or riot from being committed by the said John Short during such time as he may remain in the said house'. In his defence, it must be said that the accommodation for the Master was far from lavish, in fact closely resembling the hovels many of the inmates would have been familiar with. According to Benjamin Tucker's memories, the Master's sitting room had a sanded floor, with no carpet or common table, and the chairs had rush seats (presumably making them rather rustic in design).

Shortly afterwords, a new Master was appointed by the name of Samuel Gould, his wife Sarah being Mistress, or Matron. He asked the overseers for a piece of carpet and another chair or two, but was brusquely informed: 'No. What you have is quite sufficient.'

Mr Gould must have been a better class of incumbent but seems to have died in 1813 as *The Christchurch Times* of 1864 reports the death of his son, John. John Gould was Master for 47 years, and his obituary in the article referred to describes him as 'an old and much-esteemed inhabitant', having carried out with aplomb this post so 'commonly arduous and difficult' and earned thereby 'the fullest confidence' of the parish officers and the 'respect and esteem' of 'those committed to his charge'. And who were the people committed to his charge?

A Register of Inmates of 1811 shows that inmates were of all ages, including entire families and some who were born in the workhouse. They left if they died, 'ran off', which several did, including two children, one aged 13, the other 10; were 'sent out' - incredibly, one of the two people who left for this reason was 90; or sent to Brideswell (one person) or to Salisbury Infirmary. Many babies were born in the workhouse. A strange case is referred to in the 1824 Select Vestry Minutes: one Ann Shave, from Ringwood parish, 'having lately been delivered of a bastard child in the workhouse' was sent to the magistrate for committal to prison.

Most of these babies were illegitimate. The overseers would make efforts to seek maintenance from the supposed father in order to avoid having to maintain the child on the parish (rather as today the Child Support Agency operates!). Many original Bastardy Bonds are still kept in the Priory Church archives. These were standardised legal documents in which both parents were named, and the father, who had to sign the document, accepted responsibility for the maintenance of his child, lest it should become chargeable to the parish. An early example from 1773 cites one Mary Vatcher, 'lately delivered of a female bastard child', the father of which, one Christopher Morey, was bound over in the sum of 30 pounds 'of lawful money of Great Britain' to be paid to the overseers and churchwardens.

If a man deserted his wife and family, he was likely to find himself hauled in front of the magistrates. For example, in 1861 a saddler was sentenced to three months' hard labour for this offence. The court took the view that with his trade he was capable of earning enough to support them.

The inmates' occupations in the House at about this time are listed in other surviving records, and included spinning flax and worsted, making or mending clothes, making beads, knitting (probably of stockings, or, by the mid-18th century, gloves), digging the garden, picking hemp, and, this being the principal occupation, making fusee chains. All these occupations earned money for the parish, and thus kept down the Poor Rate. Employers in the town included William Pickford, William Goff, Charles Chisfel and James Mowlem. Some of the inmates were old or infirm and thereby exempt from employment; it would not always be so. Children were occupied in straw hat and bonnet-making, as also were 'males and females incapable of severe labour'. Robert Miller was the person thay worked for.

Of particular interest is the employment of the inmates in the making of the fusee chains - miniature chain links used in the mechanism of watches and clocks. One of the local manufacturers, Robert Harvey Cox, employed the workhouse inmates on this painstaking work from around 1800 until about 1814. Allen White, in his book *The Chain Makers*, reveals that this would have been a task largely for young girls under nine, working probably around 70 hours a week. If this was indeed the case, it should be judged by posterity as exploitation rather than any more benevolent undertaking.

17th century records held by the Priory Church list apprenticeships for the poor children from the parish and list names of the apprentices and their employers. These show that the children entered a variety of trades: the Newfoundland fishing trade accounted for some; a range of skills would have been taught others. The most unusual on record must surely be mud-wall making. Others in this period included tailoring, cordwaining (shoemaking), husbandry, housewifery and servants and mariners. Husbandry and housewifery were apparently no more than unpaid drudgery.

Some of the girls were put into service via adverts in *The Salisbury Journal* to 'creditable and respectable housekeepers', with a premium of £10 for each such person placed. This was common practice in these times, offloading a pauper child for a premium to defray parish expenses, and may well have led to abuses against Christchurch children as it was widely abused elsewhere. It was certainly the case that girls in service were usually appallingly overworked. The overseers were always conscious of the need to reduce the Poor Rate: another example was the threat issued to dispossess constant applicants for relief issued in 1824:

'Whereas several persons in this parish receiving constant relief are possessed of cottages, lands and gardens, it is agreed to propose to such poor persons that they convey their respective cottages and lands to this parish, to take effect after the death of such persons, and in the case of the refusal of those paupers to make such conveyances, on account of preserving the same for their children, the relief to those paupers to cease, as it will be expected that they shall be from that time supported by their respective children for whom such cottages and lands are preserved.' Nowadays we would call this extortion!

With schemes of this sort. it is hardly a surprise to read the Rev. Bingley's observations (History of Christchurch, 1813) that 'it is entirely from the excellent regulations adopted and persevered in . . . that the Poors' rates in the parish of Christchurch are so much lower than those of almost all the other parishes of the county.'

Another practice of the overseers was to hire out workhouse labour. The daily charge was a shilling for an able-bodied man, 10d for someone not able-bodied, and a mere 8d for a man over 60 (Select Vestry Minutes 1824).

Herbert Druitt (the *Miscellany*) attributed thriftiness to the working man, who supported the Friendly Societies as an insurance against times of want. Bingley reports that there were four of these, with a membership of 361.

Allen White (*op cit*) refers to Poor House regulations providing for the children having 10 minutes at a time reading tuition, and all inmates having two hours out of the 24 for air and exercise. In this respect, the boys had a better chance than the girls, perhaps, as they had the opportunity of a privileged education. In 1805 and 1824, the Select Vestry Minutes which survive record that eight of them could attend St Michael's School, in the Priory Loft, for free tuition in reading, writing and arithmetic.

Apart from details of occupations, the records can also tell us about other aspects of the inmates' life. They were, for instance, dressed in the earliest days in lincey coats - a rough mix of linen and wool; dowlas shifts - these were coarse calico undergarments; warper aprons and worsted hose. Inmates were generally expected to give up such clothes as they had and wear special workhouse issue, but the degree of compulsion in Christchurch at the time is not known. Benjamin Joy Tucker, in his memoirs of the early 19th century, describes the men as wearing clothing, shoes and stockings made by the inmates, the Master having cut out the clothes and shoes himself. As to their food, provisions ordered in 1768 listed beef, milk, rice, pork, peas, flour, suet, cheese, butter, beer, molasses and bread (which was to be 'best seconds' - another economy measure). The beer may seem unexpected: in 1835 the Master was authorised to buy beer for himself, his family, and 'such cases in the House as may require it'. Food was measured, men getting more than women, and children less than women.

As to how many people were in the House at any one time, numbers greatly fluctuated. The largest number to date was given to a vestry meeting as 136, in the year 1789. This would have been at the height of the Enclosure Awards' ill-effects, which led to an increase in rural poverty on account of people losing their rights to graze their animals on common land, and is certainly borne out by other records; in fact these show a steady rise from the initial 1768 figure of 62 persons to 98 at the end of 1772, 125 in 1788, 171 in 1800, then down again to under 100 throughout 1803. That is an enormous number of people to have been in the House, even allowing for the additional space in the women's wards which were demolished at the end of the 19th century. In the 'hungry forties' there were once again around 100 people. By contrast, the vestry meeting was told that, at the time, 1868, there were only 38 people, although the reasons for this will become apparent later.

This account brings the workhouse story more or less up to 1834, the date of the enormous upheaval in the philosophy of the workhouse movement, encapsulated in the great Poor Law Amendment Act, popularly known as the 'New Poor Law'. We find the town described at this time thus:

'The houses had a weather-worn tinge, dripping eaves and moss-grown tiles, if not thatch, coverings. Shops were few and of little account.' (*The Christchurch Times*, 1860; memories of a correspondent 'well-wisher'). The Tythe Map below shows how the workhouse buildings and their surroundings looked around this time.

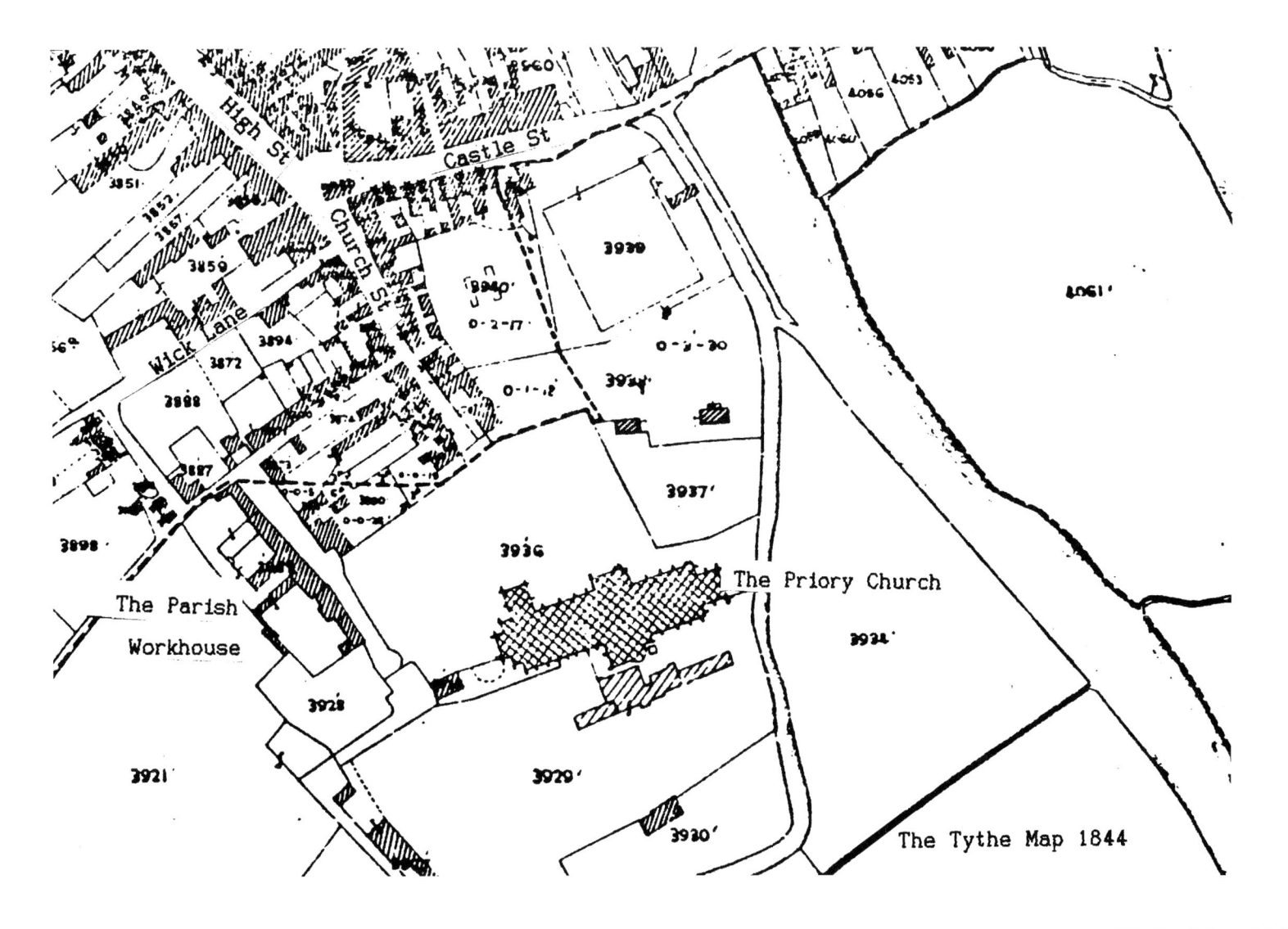

"Tythe Map 1844"

CHAPTER THREE

later years

The reasons for the implementation of this Act, which had enormous repercussions for the way workhouses were run, and which is responsible for the revulsion which the very word 'workhouse' conjures up today, were complex. There was no doubt that the existing provision was being abused, at great cost to the ratepayers, by so-called paupers living the life of Riley at the parish's expense, or intimidating overseers to obtain relief. The sheer numbers receiving relief had escalated dramatically; by 1832 around one in ten people were on relief in some way. This was not entirely the result of misuse of the system by the poor - it was a time of great social uprest occasioned by the industrial revolution, with the advent of mechanisation throwing people out of work everywhere and putting an end to the old 'cottage' industries. Reformers also wished to make a distinction between the 'deserving' and 'undeserving' poor, which in many ways still concerns society today, with the problem of 'social security scroungers', suspicion, often misplaced, of single mothers etc.

The result of the legislation was that, like it or not, parishes had to combine into 'Unions', and most of them were to build a large and grim new 'Union' workhouse, the effect of which was to deter the poor from entering by the obnoxious conditions that were enforced within. Out-relief was to be refused in all but the most deserving cases, and all applicants for relief were to be offered only the terrifying 'House'. Uniforms, hard and monotonous 'task' work, meagre rations - all these were features of the new system. But the cruellest aspect of all was the policy of separating people into 'classifications' - husbands from wives, parents from children, brothers from sisters. If one member of the family applied for relief, they all had to go in the House. If an unmarried mother asked for relief for her child, she had to go in the House together with the child. Unfortunately, this effort to deter the idle able-bodied poor very soon became the means by which the helpless old, the innocent children and the sick were harshly repressed.

The effect this legislation had on the Christchurch parish workhouse was in the first instance to require it to amalgamate with Holdenhurst and Sopley parishes. The original parish comprised the old borough, the tythings of Bure, Burton, Street, Hurn, Iford, Parley, Tuckton and Winkton, and the hamlets of Hinton Admiral, Bockhampton, Bransgore, Highcliffe and Mudeford. With the addition of Holdenhurst and the existing responsibility for Tuckton and Iford, it will be seen that the Union's area covered the future Bournemouth; thus it was always the case that the two towns shared responsibility for poor relief.

Board of Guardian Minutes show that in 1836 Ringwood and Burley parishes asked to join the Union, but their request was rejected. Had it have been allowed, perhaps the decision to keep the existing workhouse building may not have been made; perhaps the Guardians would have been obliged to build one of the grim fortress-type structures that were springing up in unions all over the country as a consequence of the Act. Evidence emerged later that the dislike felt for the idea was on account of the poverty of Ringwood. It seems that Christchurch looked down on her neighbour, and may have felt that the cost of poor relief would not have been so economical as heretofore (*The Christchurch Times,* 1878).

As a further consequence, in the words of *A Historical and Descriptive Account of the Town and Borough of Christchurch*, published very soon after the passing of the new Act in 1837, 'the Poor House has been considerably enlarged to accommodate more effectually an extra number of paupers augmented in consequence of the union of the parish with several adjacent ones'. The same Guardian Minutes quoted above do record that the Board did get approval from the Poor Law Commissioners for alterations. These included an extension, for which John Holloway won the contract.

The new law was administered at local level by the creation of a Board of Guardians. At national level it was applied by the Poor Law Commissioners until 1847, when the investigation of gross abuses at the Andover workhouse led to their replacement by the Poor Law Board. The first Board of Guardians at once agreed to introduce a classification scheme for the inmates and appointed two of their number as visitors to the workhouse to make monthly reports on its state, although this latter measure merely continued the practice of the overseers mentioned as far back as 1815. The classification scheme never seemed to materialise, although in the following year a reference appears in the Guardians' Minutes to the foundation of a new building, and another mention appears in 1845 of an addition to separate the boys from the old and infirm men (this implies that for the 11 years since the new Act, they had not been separated). 'Certain additions, alterations and repairs' were sanctioned in 1866, the Guardians' Minutes coyly mention. Further evidence for the slow progress toward classification is more clearly mentioned soon after, as the Poor Law Board began to harangue the Guardians on this point and about the disrepair of the House. There were seven main classes of people; the infirm males, infirm females, able-bodied males, able-bodied females, boys over 7 and under 16, girls over 7 and under 16, and children under 7. By the time the Poor Law Board was making these persistent complaints, numbers of inmates were regularly below 40 or so, which made it all the more ludicrous that the pressure should have been applied. It also suggests that the intention of the new Act was being fulfilled, and paupers preferred to die of starvation outside than go in, but we cannot tell for certain.

The Board of Guardians all met once a week in the office of their clerk, Henry Pain, at the workhouse, in the boardroom shown on the plan. Over the ensuing years, as the population, especially of the mushrooming new town of Bournemouth ('Holdenhurst'), grew, more Guardians were needed. In 1868 Holdenhurst got another Guardian; in 1871 a further one was elected, making Holdenhurst's representation four, and the following year Christchurch gained a seventh Guardian. When the Guardians were abolished in 1930, there were over 30 on the Board, so great was the population growth.

Whilst the workhouse had room for the paupers, eventually the boardroom could not accommodate the Guardians, and their meetings in later years were held at James Druitt's house in the High Street, now, of course, the public library.

Other well-known local names who served on the Board were Charles Hicks (also a churchwarden), James Druitt, John Edward Holloway of Hengistbury Mining Company notoriety, Mr Cooper-Dean of Little Down House and Alexander Jones. *Ex-officio* members were also on the Board for many years, e.g General Stuart and Lord Malmesbury.

The first Visitors' report on the House contained nothing more remarkable than the observation that 'the attic bedroom ceiling be taken down and the bedroom be ceiled to the rafters'.

After the death of the Master, John Gould, his assistant, Harry Heath, and his wife, Mary, were appointed at the salary of £20 plus rations. Although there were three other candidates, all with experience in the post in other unions and Mr Heath had only been an assistant for three months, he was selected. The lack of experience is also demonstrated in that he was previously a draper's assistant. But he had, reported *The Christchurch Times*, 'discharged his duties to the satisfaction of the house surgeon, the visitors, and the Rev. Nash, curate'. Whilst he was there, Mr

Heath whiled away his time building boats in the loft of a building known as 'the Net House', which was adjacent to the existing workhouse buildings on the church side, and which the Guardians purchased in 1869. The 'greatly respected' Heaths went to Sheffield Workhouse, presumably to advance their careers, in 1871. 'Their gentle manners, towards all brought into contact with them from without, combined with kindness and necessary firmness to those under their charge, bind on them the esteem of the neighbourhood they leave and the greatful respect of the inmates they tended with almost parental care', waffled *The Christchurch Times* in an echo of the praise it heaped on John Gould five years earlier. Whether this was merely diplomatic or was actually the case, we have no means of knowing.

After they left, the Guardians appointed a couple by the name of Mr and Mrs W. Clarke. There is a visiting card in an Admission book which still survives, inscribed with the name 'Mrs W. Sydenham Clarke, Melbury Lodge, Wimborne', which if it does belong to the same couple, indicates that the position of workhouse master was coming up in the world. Michael and Laura Saunderson were the holders of the posts from 1876.

CHAPTER FOUR

workhouse life

There survives from this post-New Poor Law period a little pamphlet detailing the inmates of the workhouse for the half year ending Lady Day (end of March) 1857. The statistics contained therein reveal some inklings of the inhabitants. 91 people were then in the House. The majority, 65, were from Christchurch parish, with little Sopley supplying 16 - a reflection of the level of rural poverty so common. From neighbouring Holdenhurst only six people were represented. The remaining four people are described as 'irremoveable poor'. This did not mean that they were too ill to leave the House, rather that they were from another parish but had been in the Christchurch Union the required five year period to qualify for a settlement certificate.

The booklet goes on to analyse the causes of their incarceration: 18 were infirm; four out of work (therefore, presumably able-bodied); four people had a father out of work, three of whom were from the shared surname members of one family; two had a father ill, and one had a husband also ill. So the rest of the leaflet lists social calamities of one sort or another as the cause: 14 children were possessed of a mother whose 'misconduct' was responsible for their plight; a further three children's mother had deserted them, four children were deserted by their father. This group tells a story - four children in one family in the workhouse were deserted by the father, and the mother was also in the House on account of her husband's 'misconduct'. These family tragedies were supplemented by a mixed group of misfits, chiefly represented by eight inmates admitted for 'misconduct', of whom it is notable that they were all female, which gives some clue to the nature of the misconduct, perhaps. One of these, Eliza Pack, aged 29, had been 95 days in the workhouse on account of her misconduct, together with her five children. As the last one was stated to be aged 3 months, it may have been born in the workhouse. Three children were orphans. Five 'idiots', one insane (also guilty of 'misconduct'), one 'out of place' (another settlement category, probably awaiting removal to the parish of origin), and a further four who were ill, illustrating a role for the workhouse of aiding the sick. This role is further corroborated by a newspaper account for the same year, though a couple of months after these records, of the tragic case of a terrible accident at the Hengistbury Mining Company works. One of the workers sustained such a serious head injury that his brain was protruding beyond the skull. Still conscious, he was removed from the Head and taken to the workhouse.

To complete the statistics, one vagrant is listed. Either what was to become a major problem for the authorities had not yet become one, or there were not yet the penalties for sleeping out in the open that such people later endured. Later statistics show that, in one week in 1880, there were between two and six vagrants in the workhouse. They were hardly encouraged, their food allowance consisting of half a pound of bread at night and the same in the morning. The protests that became a common feature of the vagrants' wards in the new workhouse were already in evidence: a tramp who refused to do his work and then tore up his clothes was sentenced to seven weeks in jail for his trouble in 1878.

It was frequently the case that children, especially babies, were abandoned at the workhouse door. An advert appears in 1873 in *The Christchurch Times* offering a £10 reward for information leading to the conviction of the person who deposited one such baby at the House - a boy of around 18 months age.

A large proportion of the inmates had been there, according to this record, for the entire period of 182 days, indicating that there were many long-stay cases.

The same informative little pamphlet lists the current Guardians: W. W. Farr (nicknamed by Benjamin Tucker 'Old Far and Near'), George Aldridge, Edward Sleat Elliott, James Taylor, Richard Dale, Herbert Plowman, Charles Clarke, Lieut. Col. Simmonds, James Aldridge, Henry Bone and Mr Whicher. The last two represented Sopley and remained in office for many years; Mr Whicher was a farmer who lived at Throop House. Messrs Simmonds and J. Aldridge represented Holdenhurst. (Another Bournemouth Guardian around this time was the Rev. A. M. Bennett, described by Mary Graham in her book *The Royal National Hospital* as that town's first vicar, also responsible for the building of many Bournemouth churches, a 'serious, dedicated man'.) William Farr lived at Iford House - long since vanished - and was a JP.

The officers were:

Mr A. Q. Palmer, Surgeon (salary £70);

Mr R. S. J. Stevens, also Surgeon (£70);

Mr H. Pain, Clerk to the Guardians (£50);

Mr J. Gould, Master (£20);

Miss Sarah Gould, Matron (£20);

Mr S. Bemister, Relieving Officer (£70);

Mr H. Pain, Clerk to Overseers (£40);

Miss Gould, Schoolmistress (£32).

Mr H Pain was a busy man, holding two public posts, or, more likely, one of the 'H. Pain's above was in fact his son, also H. Pain. The second H. Pain was appointed clerk the year after this, in 1858 'in the room of his late lamented father' (*The Christchurch Times*). This H. Pain was also an assistant overseer, which seems to identify him with the second Pain above. He continued in the post until 1876, when he resigned in favour of James Druitt. Mr Druitt became a Guardian in later years.

Mr Samuel Bemister was one of the many notable Christchurch people connected with the affairs of the workhouse. Seven times mayor of the town, his public service was commemorated by a fountain, now reinstated near its original position at Fountain roundabout.

This is the first mention of the school. On the plan, it is shown where the costume gallery is now housed, with a yard for the boys on one side, and the girls' yard on the other. Miss Lucinda Gould, another of what seems to have been a virtual dynasty of Goulds, had, says *The Christchurch Times*, been the schoolmistress for almost 28 years. She died in 1871. If she died in office, this would set the date for the school back to at least 1843, very early on in an age before compulsory education, although the schools were not necessarily renowned for instruction in this period. At least Christchurch Workhouse did not delegate the task to an inmate, as was done in many other unions, where it was not unusual for the children to be subject to great cruelty. The article describes her as a 'useful and painstaking public servant'. Her replacement was a Miss Nunn, though she resigned after a year (marriage?), succeeded by a Miss Martha James, who stayed in the post just two years, next a Miss Clara Langley, who lasted a mere eight months, then a Miss Emily Hales followed. She was given a report of 'satisfactory performance' by a Poor Law Board school inspector in 1877. Three years later she quarrelled with another member of the school staff, who deemed herself 'ill-used' by the lady.

Children generally stayed on until they gained their certificates, which took some of them longer than others. Then the girls could be released into service.

There is evidence for ill-treatment of the children. In 1881 (when the children were at Tuckton temporarily, for reasons that will be given), a woman by the name of Elizabeth Collis described as the 'housekeeper of the school of Christchurch Union' appeared before local magistrates charged with assaulting Elizabeth Brine, a child at the school. She claimed she was not in the habit of beating the children at all, but her claim was met by laughter in the court. She was given a 5s penalty and she and her husband left their employment shortly afterwards. At least this shows that mistreatment was not ignored.

When not engaged in some form of study (in 1880 this took up three hours of their time each day), the pauper children were occupied as usual assisting around the House. Girls helped the women in scrubbing, boys helped the men garden, although the Guardians were not at all happy for the adults to mix with the children. The 'loose women' - presumably this is another clue to the 'misconduct' for which so many were admitted - 'polluted the minds' of the girls and led to their 'ruination'. Another effect of the absence of a proper classification system.

A new destiny for boys is mentioned in 1875 - the Guardians went to Southampton to inspect a training ship. A life at sea became a common prospect for workhouse boys for many years to come.

The adults continued to be gainfully employed - picking horsehair was a new and tedious task added to the previous list. Their diet seemed to be similar, but tea and bacon appear on a 1868 dietary and coffee by 1878. As always, obedience was strictly enforced: one able-bodied man got a pound of potatoes instead of a pound of pudding for refusing to attend church - and then three weeks in jail for refusing to work. The advert asking for tenders for the workhouse provisions had the ominous item: 'Coffins (elm board three-quarters of an inch thick, free of knots. Pitched handles, screws and wool)'.

One group of inmates not previously mentioned is the 'frankly named 'lunatics'. These people were from the early days sent to asylums: Fisherton House, near Salisbury, being one, and the Hampshire County Asylum at Knowle, Fareham, being another. In 1857, eight such people were maintained by the parish at Fareham. 'Imbeciles' were still accommodated at the workhouse. One such person is described in Benjamin Tucker's memoirs in the time of Harry Heath and incidentally gives us some information about sanitary conditions:

'The water for the use of the House was dipped up at the quay into a barrel and wheeled to the premises by a half-witted man, whose name was Charlie Chisel, and who also blew the bellows for the organist at church. On one occasion, after the service was over, Miss Tullock (the organist) said to Charlie: "Didn't I play well today?" The next Sunday the organist could not play until she told Charlie that it was he who helped her to do so well. [This man was not as stupid as he seemed!] The organ at that time was on the Rood Screen, and I used to sit in a pew with my cousins by the side of it and give Charlie pieces of tallow candle, which he ate.

'At the workhouse, in a cell facing south, a lunatic by the name of Jones was chained to a post in the rear; in fine weather the door was kept open and he could be seen crouched on his haunches and singing "I'm going to, London, to London. I'm going to London."

'Knowing one of the sons of the Master, I often went with him to see Jones, and I regret to say we sometimes teased him, but woe betide the person who got within his spring.'

Why such a poor soul as this was not in an asylum is not clear. It could be that Fareham asylum was full, as were many others in these times. It certainly was in 1879, and asked the Christchurch Guardians to take back their 'harmless' patients, but were told that there was no room for them back in the workhouse either. A visit by The Commissioners in Lunacy produced a report on the old building in 1881 that the 'accommodation is so bad [that it is] not suitable or adequate for any class of the insane [on account of] defective premises'. These poor afflicted people would have been confined in the same wards as sane people - an intolerable state of affairs.

A notorious case of abuse to an inmate of an asylum - Fisherton House in this case - is detailed in letters held in the Christchurch Library Local History Room and also appears in *The Christchurch Times* in 1878. A young lady, German by birth, was hired as a servant by a lady then staying in Bournemouth. She was soon found to be insane, and her employer sent her to this asylum, which was then managed by two doctors by the name of Finch and Lush. After a few weeks, her employer not unreasonably refused to continue to maintain her ex-employee. On receiving this intelligence, Dr Lush tried without success to persuade the Christchurch Guardians to take her. They said she was the responsibility of the Fisherton parish. Two or three weeks later, the lady was dumped unceremonially by the side of a road in Bournemouth, on the instructions, it was implied, of Dr Lush. She was taken by the police to the Fareham asylum, where she was maintained by the Christchurch Guardians whilst the settlement arguments continued. This is a fine example of the horrors of the settlement system and the way the helpless poor could be treated by those responsible for their welfare. The Guardians called Dr Lush's action 'highly improper', which it was, to say the least.

Another asylum, Nazareth House, was frequently used for children, but there were also many other names that appear over the years, e.g. The Western Counties Idiot Asylum at Starcross in Exeter and another in Chichester.

Life had its small pleasures for these people, from time to time. The most well-known occasion for celebration is, of course, Christmas, when they were treated to a traditional meal served by or at least attended by the Guardians. The first reference to this appears in 1867. On New Year's Day, the borough's MP, Admiral Walcott, treated them to a dinner. One Mr Kerley of Bournemouth, probably the same person who was a Bournemouth Guardian, gave the sum of 10s to be spent on nuts and oranges for the youngsters, soup and tobacco for their elders. In 1872, the clerk to the Guardians, James Druitt, and the wife of Guardian Holloway set up a fund to raise money for 'some good cheer' for the inmates. Another benefactor was the Hon. Miss Wrottesley.

The curate, later vicar, of Christchurch, the Rev. Z. Nash, became a frequent benefactor, every year treating the inmates to a tea. In 1880, this consisted of 'ham, bread and butter, plum and seedcake etc', and personal gifts of buns and oranges and 'sundry other gifts'. Particularly appreciated would have been the half pound of tea to each old woman, and doubtless the same appreciation would have been felt by the old men for their tobacco. The Rev. Pretyman of Bournemouth was another sincere and generous benefactor, and a Guardian for many years. It would be hard to over-emphasise the value that the children in particular would have placed on these rare opportunities to leave their dull confinement, where they would have been unlikely to have had any possessions, let alone toys, and mix with a normal family.

There seemed to be usually about 50 to 70 people in the House in the 1850s, but the number dwindled, and in the 1860s was often hovering around 40. These pathetic inmates were apparently comprised of all those who could not avoid the new-style workhouse: in the words of Guardian George Aldridge, 'the great majority of inmates are of naturally weak or disordered intellect - of previously immoral life, or of aged persons far advanced in second childhood. Of the children, many inherit vicious tendencies. A Master and Mistress, more kind and gentle than many parents, are taxed to their utmost.' (1867. The Heaths were in residence.) This assessment indicates that the able-bodied were indeed being deterred, as the New Poor law Act intended, from entering the workhouse, but unfortunately the other categories had no choice. 'Aged persons' seemed positively welcomed in the workhouse. An 1879 boardroom proposal that all those over 70 and living alone 'should have the privilege of going into the poorhouse where they could be better looked after' received general assent.

The conditions that were experienced by the inmates began to ease up by the time 30 or so years had elapsed since the 1834 Act. This is borne out by the remark of George Aldridge to a vestry meeting: 'The Poor Law system has improved of late years, and it was necessary that the morality of the inmates should be looked after in a better way than had formerly been the case.'

CHAPTER FIVE

the end of the old workhouse

1867 and 1868 mark the years when the future of the workhouse's present building was weighed in the balance and found wanting, and the date from which the long search for alternative premises began.

Christchurch was still a small and inconsequential place at this time. 'Christchurch consists for the most part of one long straggling street with in many places long intervals between the houses', a letter from the Guardians to the Local Government Board bemoans in 1875. But, Bournemouth, of course, was in quite a different league. In the words of one of the Guardians: 'Forty years ago, Bourne was a mere stream, but now it was as broad as the Thames of London'. The Guardians estimated that the housing stock of Bournemouth was being increased by about 200 houses a year.

As mentioned previously, the predecessor to the Local Government Board, the Poor Law Board, had been reproaching the Guardians about the workhouse for some time. Little details were leaking out to *The Christchurch Times* - at this time and until 1877 no reporters could attend the Board meetings. News that the House was condemned by the Poor Law Board as 'inconvenient', was nevertheless reported in 1867, as was the news that the Poor Law Board had threatened the Guardians with an order to build a new workhouse if they did not enlarge the present one. When the Guardians did present a plan for enlarging the buildings, the Poor Law inspectors insisted on a new one being erected; furthermore, if they did not comply, the Board would force the amalgamation of the Christchurch Union with that of Ringwood.

A vestry meeting to discuss the matter was called - the workhouse building was still owned by the overseers. The Guardians sought to purchase the buildings for themselves, and they were eventually successful in doing so, thereby at least gaining control of the workhouse buil... in 1868, it was revealed that the Poor Law inspector ha... House repeatedly, on the grounds of absence or insufficiency... the dilapidated state of the buildings and the confined site. T... pointed out that it was absurd to try to classify 40 or so occupants 28 different divisions, and showed some compassion to the inn... remarking: 'The present inmates of the House were only like a fam... there were any couples, why not treat them liberally and let them live ou... the House?' It is only to be hoped that Mr Druitt's suggestion was taken up, and that old couples were no longer separated, if at all they were. Mr Aldridge compared Christchurch Workhouse with other named local unions, and confidently pronounced it to be the best. Classification, said Mr Druitt, was 'wholly inapplicable to the circumstances' of their union. After heated exchanges (particularly between George Aldridge and Elias Lane) and meetings that were several times adjourned, the vestry resolved to allow the overseers to sell the workhouse buildings to the Board of Guardians for £600. At the next election, George Aldridge declined to be nominated, and James Druitt took his place.

By 1871, it was apparent that the Guardians had merely patched up the building to save any expense to the ratepayers that they could. They were often torn between these two loyalties, although their priority should always have been the poor. It must have been then, as it is today, a hard balancing act. The Guardians acknowledged that on the present site they had no room for further wards, and decided to take the opportunity of the Portfield enclosure being made at that time to keep their eyes open for a new site. The news in the local paper of this development led to a correspondent not

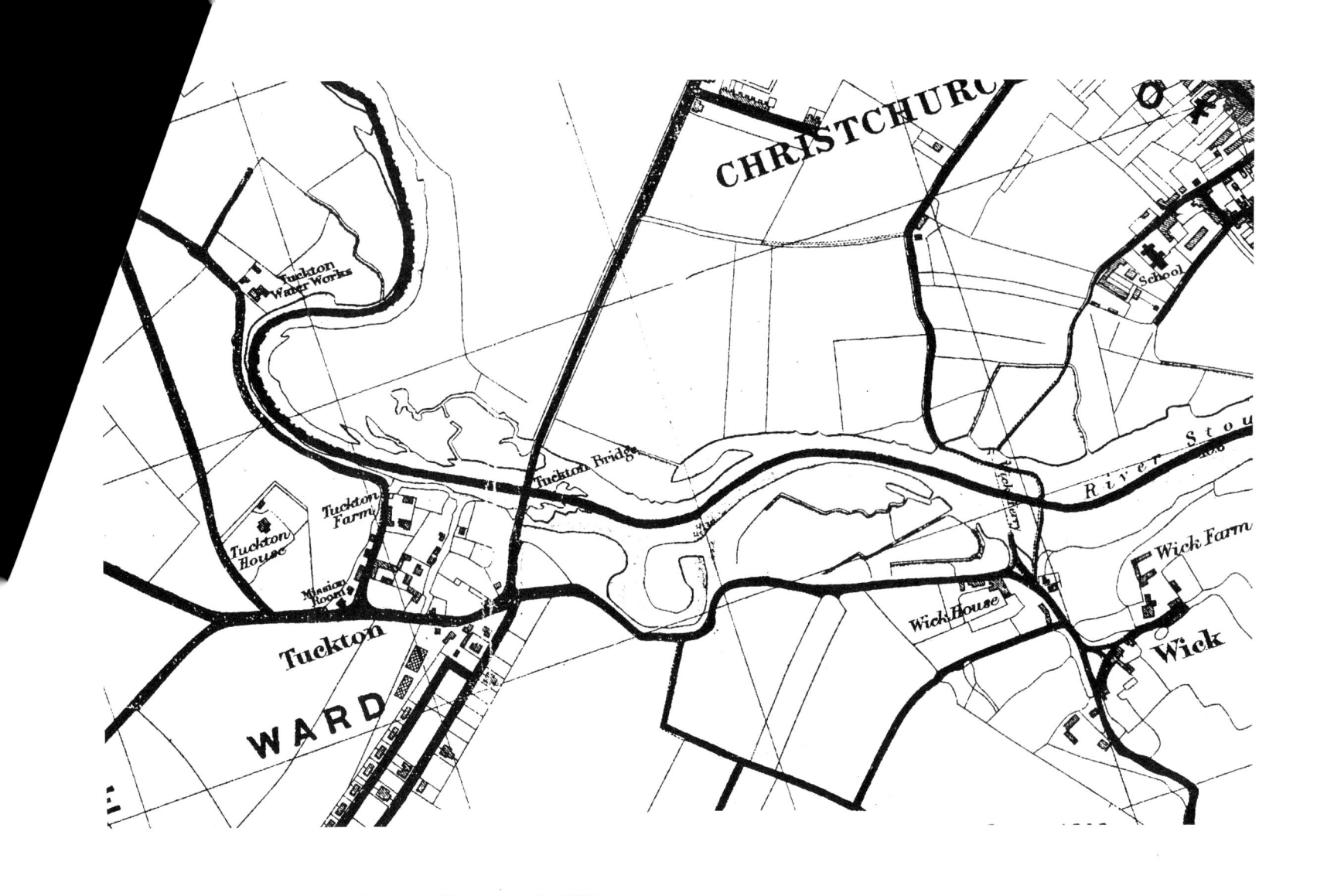

A map of Tuckton showing farm -"Bright's map of Bournemouth 1903"

unreasonably writing to enquire why, given that the workhouse once held nearly 200 inmates, room could not now be found for 60. No reply was received, but the need for separating the inmates into the required classifications was undoubtably the reason. It was no longer acceptable to mix the ages as had been the practice for so long.

Amidst the vestry squabbles, another row was looming, and it led to a Poor Law Enquiry. The Union's Medical Officer, one Dr Morril, had complained that he was being frustrated by the workhouse officials. The Relieving Officer, Samuel Bemister, responsible for the administration of out-relief, kept altering the doctor's order forms and refused to pay for wine he had ordered for his pauper patients. Mr Bemister had also, said the doctor, asked 'improper' questions in obstetric cases. The doctor also accused the Clerk, Mr Pain, of delaying his salary payments and vaccination fees, altering figures in his contract regarding additional vaccination fees, and interfering with his orders. The Guardians made counter-accusations of discourteous conduct, failure to reply to letters, and making unfounded complaints.

After hearing the evidence at length from both sides, the inspector found for the Guardians, with the small proviso that Mr Bemister should not have altered the doctor's orders, and invited the doctor's resignation . . .

The belief in the efficacy of alcohol as a medicine seems odd today but was quite orthodox then. One aged lady in the workhouse was prescribed a pint of wine a week and had been so for several years. 'It must have been an ineffectual sort of medicine,' Elias Lane drily remarked.

A turnaround in the numbers situation arose suddenly in the 1870s after the low figures of the previous decades, and did more than any Poor Law inspector to persuade the Guardians of the need for a new workhouse. The Guardians wrote to the Local Government Board in 1878 that the workhouse was full, and not only were they being forced to give out-relief when they otherwise would not (much to the literal relief, I suspect, of the recipients), but they were considering sending the children out of the House to a vacant property owned by a member of the Board. This was Frederick Moser, who resided at Carbery House, in Southbourne, a house long since demolished.

It was to his property, a farm in Tuckton, that most of the children duly went, with their schoolmistress (see map below and photo). No thought appeared to have been given to those of the children who were thereby separated from one or both parent inmates. It was very crowded even here: the children slept two to a bed. Nevertheless, It must have been a welcome change as Tuckton was then entirely rural in character.

Those with a sharp eye will have noticed that the firm of Peek's in Iford Lane is in a building far older than its neighbours; it is, in fact, the last remaining building of Tuckton Farm. The barn had a later claim to fame, being the place where Mr Rolls assembled the aircraft in which he died at the fateful 1910 air show at Hengistbury Head.

Architects' Layout for the Site, 1879

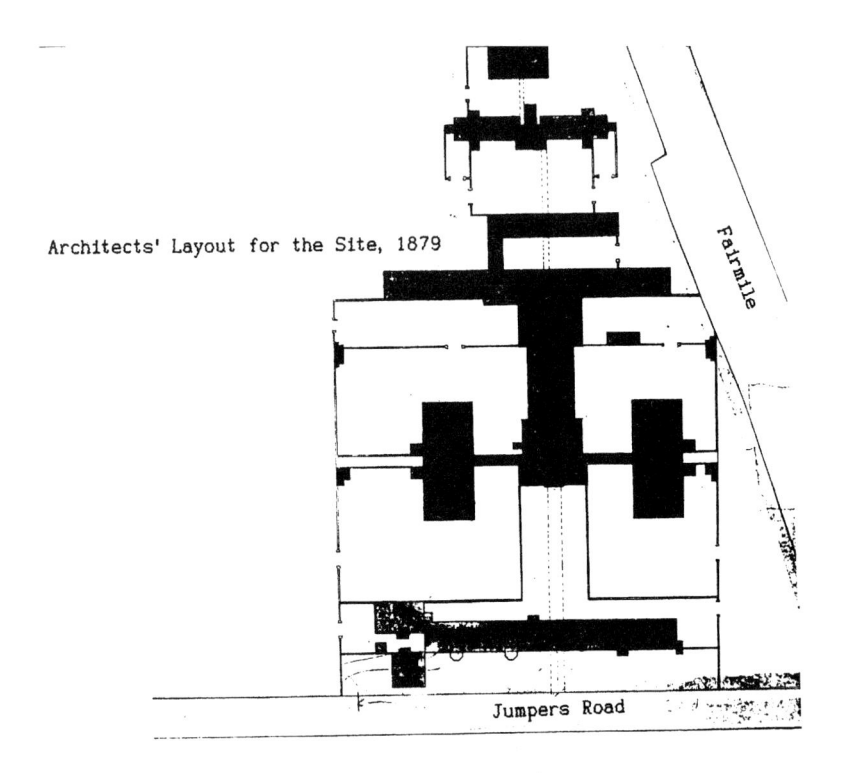

The Guardians now set about with vigour to find a new site, and much of their time over the next few years was taken up with the extraordinary palaver that accompanied these attempts. Buying the land was one thing; getting the architects to design a new building proved to be quite another. They were now feeling the pressure of the population growth: claims on the Union had doubled even within the last few months.

They first of all plumped for a site near the railway line, presumably somewhere in Portfield, but later started to purchase piecemeal parcels of land at Fairmile on which the new House was eventually built. Some of it was bought from small landowners after a suitable period of haggling: £600 to a Mr E Davis here; £150 to a Mr Budden there. Lord Malmesbury and Sir G. Gervis parted with some of their acreage, as did Sir George Meyrick. The Board purchased more than their actual requirements as their original intention was to build an isolation hospital, after selling the surplus to the Christchurch Sanitary Authority, but this never materialised (being eventually constructed in Marsh Lane). By late in 1877, the land acquisitions had been completed - at least for the initial buildings that went up; as will be seen, much more was later acquired.

Messrs Creeke and Burton were appointed architects at the beginning of 1877 - Christopher Crabbe Creeke being very well known in Bournemouth, as that town's Improvement Commissioners' first surveyor and thus responsible for the road layouts. He also designed the Central Pleasure Gardens and two wings of the Royal Bath Hotel. With this eminent firm in charge of the design work, everything seemed ready to proceed without undue hitches.

But it was not to be.

In May of that year, the Guardians were expressing their 'extreme dissatisfaction' to the architects for the delay in the completion of their plans. By October, their impatience had increased. In February 1878, James Druitt, the Clerk, issued them with an ultimatum. One or the other of the architects then attended board meetings with their plans, but were infuriatingly inconsistent in this, leading Mr Farr to accuse the pair of being 'either utterly incompetent or thoroughly neglectful'. Eventually, they decided to dispense with the architects, but did not carry out this threat, and, in fact, Edgar Burton went on to design most of the subsequent workhouse buildings. Both Creeke and Burton developed illnesses during the design stage, which further delayed proceedings.

The plans proved to be too ambitious. The Local Government Board suggested that the children's wards were omitted, on grounds of cost. A scheme for a clock tower above the entrance way was abandoned, as was the bakery. The infirmary was also postponed. When the Guardians chose the lowest tender for building from Henry Blachford of Bournemouth, for £11,865, Mr Baldwyn Fleming, the Local Government Board inspector overseeing operations, warned them that Mr Blachford must have made a grave miscalculation. His estimate was £2,000 less than the next nearest tender, but the Guardians, as they were often later to do, rejected his advice and accepted the tender. The capacity of the new House was finally decided upon as 200.

Even when the plans were in front of them, the Guardians could not have looked them over very carefully, as they were full of complaints as the building was going up. The vagrants wards were disgraceful, they said: a zinc roof, open gratings on the floor, no heating - the Guardians expressed themselves 'horror-stricken at the wretchedness with which [the vagrants] had been provided.' There was no provision for fires, the coal hole was 'a ridiculous place', said Mr Holloway, 'only capable of holding about two tons', and he had 'never seen a place so ill-adapted for the purpose required as this was. There were pumps that could never be used at all, all in the wrong places, and with no troughs to them, and many other out-of-the-way things,' he continued. The architect blamed the clerk of works for 'irregularities' on his certificates for payment, and soon became so ill he could no longer supervise the construction, and so on.

It is possible that all these difficulties arose from the fact that the great boom in workhouse construction had long gone; the Christchurch Guardians were attempting an ambitious scheme nearly fifty years after the New Poor Law era of the 1830s. As a result, the new workhouse design was a radical departure from its predecessors, reflecting attempts to find new solutions to the accommodation requirements. The resulting buildings are therefore most unusual in terms of workhouse layout.

However, eventually, all was ready and kitted out for the new occupiers. Plain, substantial well-made furniture was chosen, with a careful watch on unnecessary expense.

The big day arrived on August 23rd 1881. The first inmates were able to walk under the archway entrance in Jumpers Road and take up residence in the wards especially built to segregate the ages and sexes on either side of the grandiose quarters for the Master and Matron. They gathered in the dining hall to hear the chairman of the Board of Guardians, Mr James Kemp-Welch, tell them that 'workhouses are a necessary evil, but in the Christchurch Union everything was done for the comfort of the inmates which a kind Master and Matron could do'. A 'substantial meat tea', reported *The Christchurch Times*, 'was given to the inmates to mark the occasion,' at the chairman's expense. This included half a pound of tea for the females and a quarter of a pound of tobacco for the males. Music and readings, no doubt of a suitably elevating nature, followed.

The reality was somewhat different. The Board knew that they now had the premises with which to comply with all the requirements of classification that the Local Government Board had demanded, and that this would have an effect on their relief policy. 'The new workhouse', said the chairman to the Board, 'offered the greater facility which they would have for encouraging thrift among the poorer classes, by offering the House in many cases where they now granted outdoor relief'. He stated that he would not advocate 'harsh change' in this matter but 'one should gradually but certainly change the present system, and at all times to treat persons with careful habits differently from those who were more careless.' These words sounded very ominous - 1834 had arrived in Christchurch by 1881.

Whilst the building of the new House was being attended to, the Guardians also had to deal with the problems of the existing one. The children were still at Tuckton, although that was so cramped that some had to remain at the old workhouse, doing virtually nothing as their teacher was with the other children. There was some discussion of adapting the new buildings to accommodate them by dividing up wards, but Inspector Fleming's advice was taken on this occasion - such a scheme would spoil the appearance of the new building, scupper the all-important classification plans, and expose the children once again to the 'baneful' influence of the more incorrigible adults. Alternative arrangements had to be made.

Ideas considered included keeping the old House exclusively for the children. This was ruled out as the value of the building and its potential for reducing the debt incurred from the loan was too tempting. Perhaps half of the workhouse could be converted for their use and the other half sold. This too was rejected as impracticable. In the end, the Guardians set about adapting the old empty House for the children and their schoolteacher. Prior to making the alterations, Mr Kemp-Welch took a look around it and declared that: 'I have never in my lifetime seen a place I was so ashamed of . . . It is an astonishing thing that it had been occupied for so long.' The outer wings of the decrepit building were closed down, and the area in the middle - corresponding to the approximate area of the present museum - was patched up for the children.

Meanwhile, the Rev. Pretyman visited the children at Tuckton in 1880, and expressed himself pleased with their acadamic attainments. He also exhibited the compassion that some of the Guardians were undoubtably motivated by. Reporting back to the Board, he attempted to persuade them that it was not the fault of the children that they were in the workhouse, and the experience could 'prey on their minds in years to come'. Such revolutionary thoughts did not agree with Mr Waterfield, the then chairman, who dismissed such nonsense as unwelcome 'sentimentality'. The workhouse children were, he said, 'paupers after all that was said about them', and he would not accept that they felt any more disgrace than did those children on out-relief.

The children returned from the farm in October 1881. The old workhouse was to remain their 'home' again for another five years.

CHAPTER SIX

the Red House

The children finally joined their former fellow-inmates when their accommodation was completed in 1886.

The Guardians then pressed ahead with the sale of their old building, which by then was exceedingly dilapidated. At auction, it was sold for £825 to the Rev. T. H. Bush, vicar of the Priory Church. The bidding was hotly contested by others, amongst whom were Samuel Bemister, the Relieving Officer, a Guardian, Henry West Jenkins, and, oddly, Mr Blachford, the builder of the new workhouse!

A clue to the sight that the old House must have presented to its new owner is evident in the remark of Guardian Elias Lane after the sale, that this would be perhaps the right time to ask that the tipping of stone and refuse material against its walls be discontinued. 'It not only looked disgraceful,' he said, 'but considerably narrowed the road near the church.' He did not, he said, like to see the place so neglected as it was in this respect.

The Rev. Bush demolished the women's wards, kitchen and stores to the east of the present building, which were apparently about to fall down unaided, having been out of use for five years. Also to go was the Net House in which Mr Heath repaired his boats. In their place, the Rev. Bush built the stone wall fronting the road. In place of the hospital wing on the other side he built stables, now used as the art gallery. Another section to go was the laundry rear extension, on the site of which the vicar built a greenhouse; traces of the whitewash remain today.

So, the present museum building represents approximately half of the original set of buildings, and was renamed by its new owner as the Red House.

The Rev. Bush kept the Red House as the family home until his death in 1909. It was then purchased by the Druitt family and came into the hands of Herbert Druitt, the well-known local antiquarian, in 1916. Local directories record that H. E. Miller, a verger at the Priory, who was also a keen amateur photographer, lived in the Red House at this period - ceretainly from 1909 until at least 1913.

During this period, its ultimate role as a museum was foreshadowed by its use for the public exhibition of Mr Druitt's extensive collection of local artefacts - from 1919 to around 1923 it was occasionally opened for this purpose. But its primary function for Mr Druitt was as one of his many stores.

It was his wish that the house should become a museum, but through the apparent intransigence of the local authority this was not realised until after his death when his sister, Charlotte, gave the Red House to the town in 1947.

The first task of the trustees was to clear the enormous collection: in some parts of the ground floor it was literally holding up the ceiling! No work appeared to have been done to maintain the building, now nearly 200 years old. The roof leaked, the windows were broken and the garden heavily overgrown. It took three years to get the Red House to a state where it could fulfil Charlotte Druitt's legacy, since when this lovely building has become one of our town's greatest assets, a far cry from its humble origins, yet, in its own way, still fulfilling a need for the local populace.

CHAPTER SEVEN

the new workhouse

Back in the sprawling new premises, the Guardians held their first meeting in the new boardroom. This was not where the present one is, but closer to the archway. Whilst they were still relatively few in number, it was quite sufficient.

There was, not unnaturally, a considerable amount of mutual back-slapping at their achievement, and they all seem to have forgotten the grievances they had whilst the buildings were under construction. 'Every accommodation for the Guardians . . . excellent and convenient provision for the press . . . remarkable fitness for the purpose for which [the workhouse] had been erected', were just some of the remarks made before they settled down to hear the chairman's speech. 'The old Select Vestry system', he began, 'administered the Poor Law relief, and money was given in lieu of wages. The labourers demanded this as their right and often relief was given out of fear. To alter this state of things the Act of 1834 became a necessity.' He explained that since those days men could not simply desert their families in the knowledge they would get parish relief, as both he and the family would be put in the workhouse. The implication was that the extra space would allow the Guardians to apply these rules much more strictly.

Early Buildings

The map below shows the original group of buildings that was constructed in the first twenty years of the new workhouse.

In 1881, the components of the group which welcomed the Red House inmates are described below.

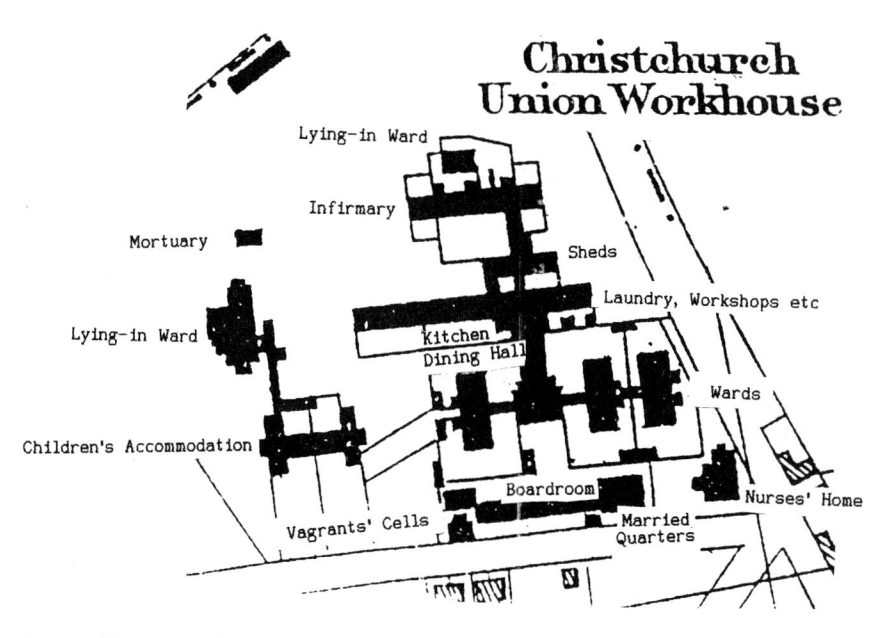

From Bright's Map of Bournemouth, 1903

The vagrants cell wards are situated to the left of the entrance row, and was extended substantially on later occasions as the numbers of vagrants increased with the growth of Bournemouth.

Note the married quarters provision for two couples. The male vagrant wards have six 'cells', with cubicles adjacent in which they had to do the day's 'task' in return for the night's shelter and food, such as it was. The task was stone-breaking, and was exceptionally hard work, deliberately so in accordance with the workhouse policy of deterrence. This facility is omitted from the female wards. They would have had another task, such as picking oakum. The disinfectant stove was for the vagrants' clothing. Note the baths: it was compulsory to be bathed on admittance. Also shown on the plans and still to be seen today are the yards, again strictly separated for males and females.

This is the archway that all inmates would have entered by, flanked on the left by the porter's lodge to whom they would have had to report, and on the right by the boardroom and clerk's office. The boardroom was later rebuilt on the site of the married couples' quarters. The architects had originally designed a clock tower for the entrance, but this was dropped on grounds of cost.

This graceful house, carefully positioned to supervise the Jumper's Road (original) entrance, was the quarters for the Master and Matron. The extension to the right was a later addition to provide a strongroom and further accommodation over.

Vagrants cell wards

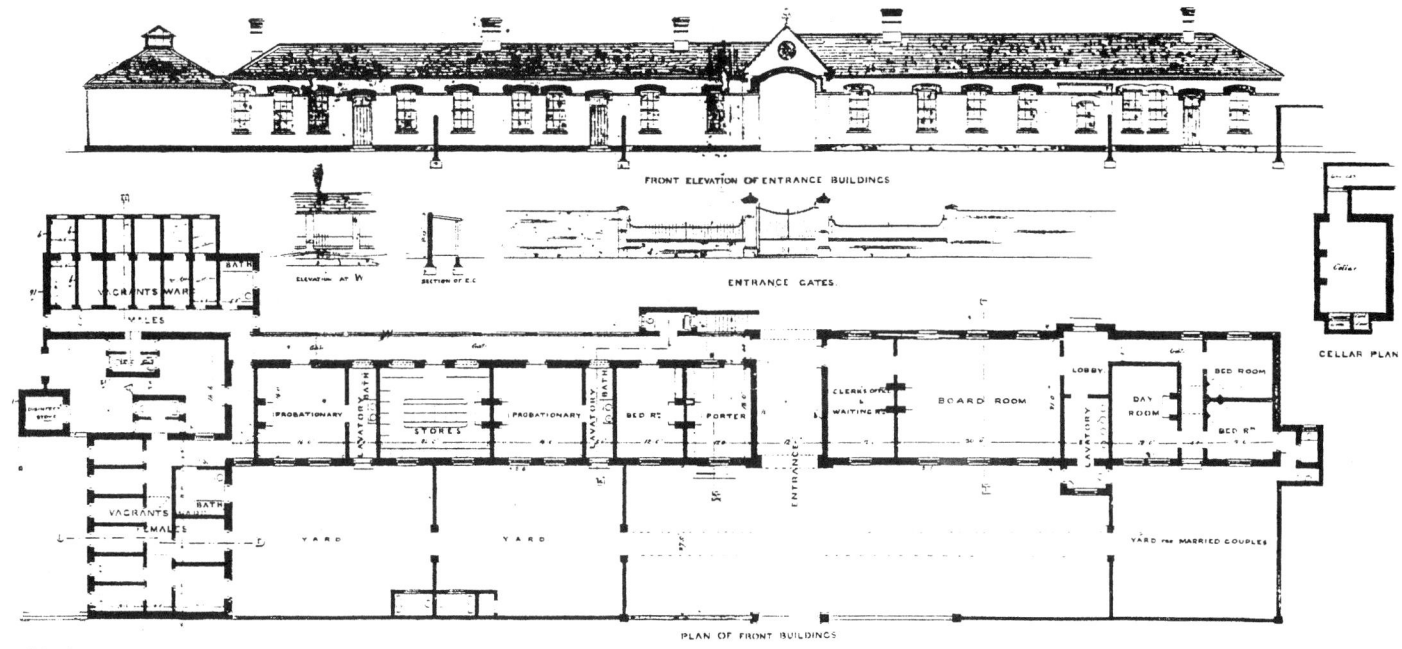

The Entrance block

There are three sets of wards, the set on the extreme right having been added in 1895 in identical design to the 1881 original. They were linked by corridor to the Master and Matron's quarters and through there to the inmates' dining hall beyond.

The Wards flanking the Master's House; female wing in foreground. Original pump just visible against yard wall.

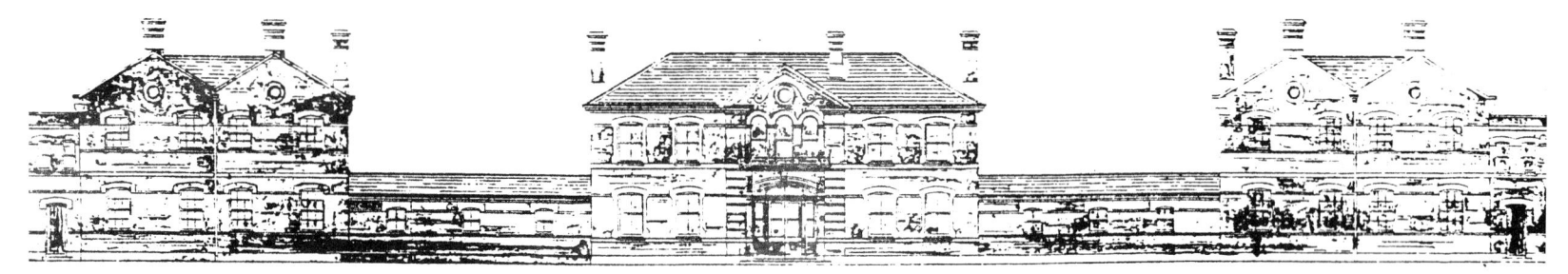

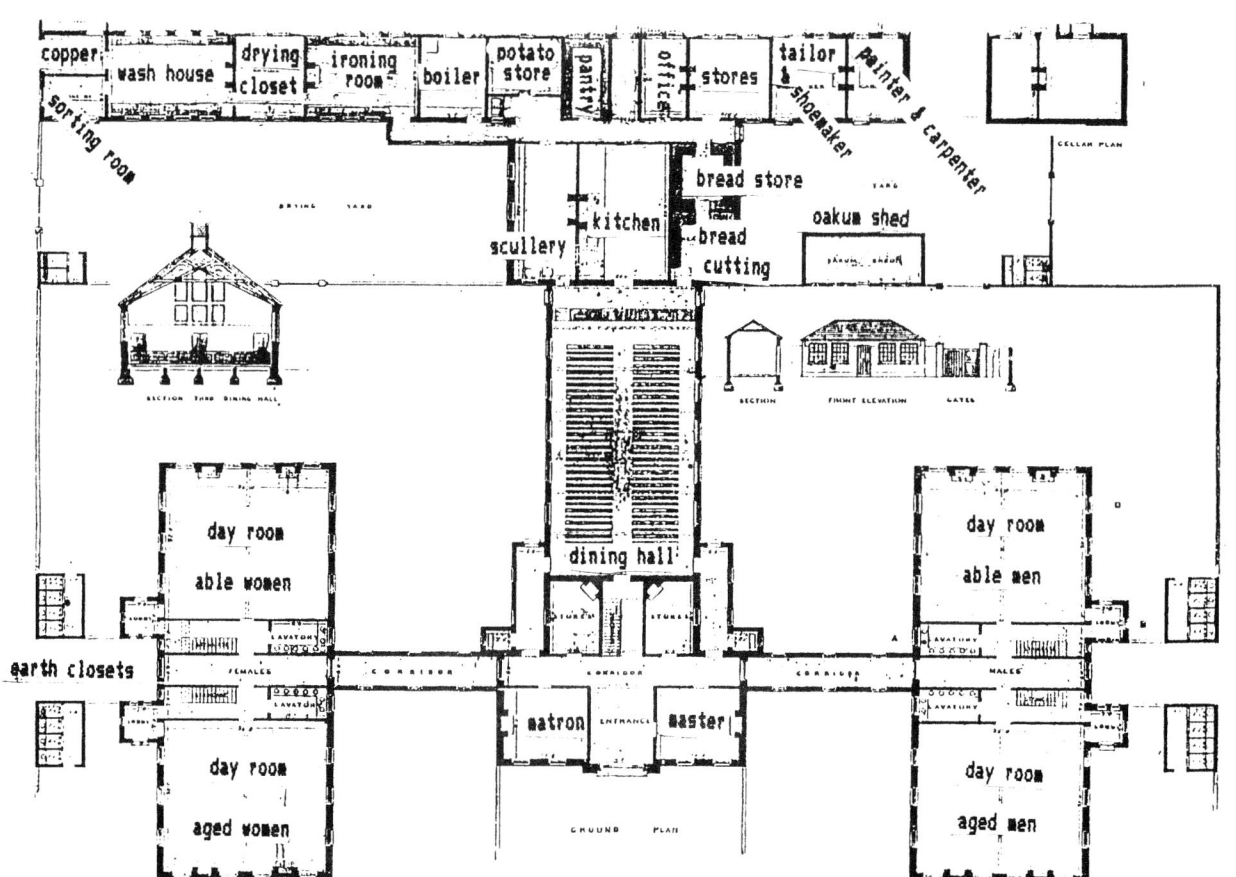

Master's House and Wards, interconnected by corridor – Front elevation.

CHRISTCHURCH UNION

As this shows, the classification system had the desired effect of separating the able-bodied from the aged, men from women (therefore husbands from wives; the married quarters were only for certain categories, e.g. the over 60s). The kitchen and stores are at the rear: note the tradesmen's workshops. Of particular interest in this plan is the oakum shed in the yard of the able-bodied men. Another example of the deterrent principle, this was tedious work separating tarred and tangled rope, often leading to bleeding fingers.

These buildings were later supplemented by the following:

The Infirmary, this was constructed the year after the first buildings.

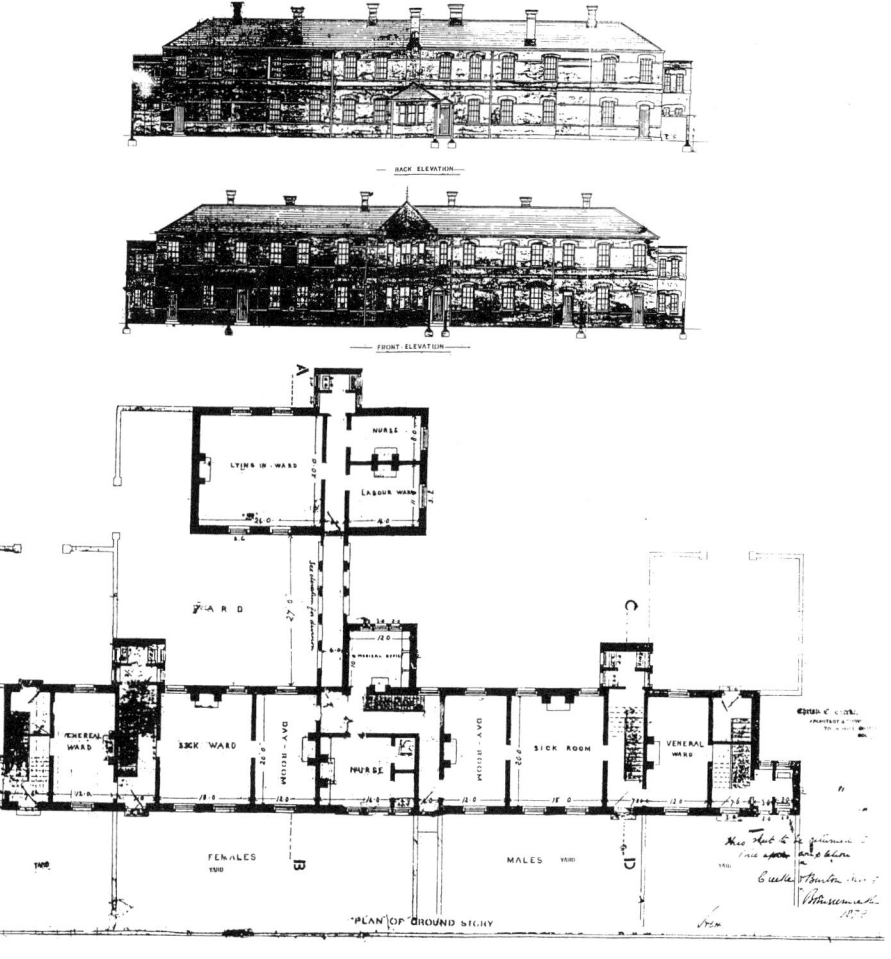

The Infirmary – Ground Floor

Note the wards for venereal disease and the male and female yards. The lying-in ward was for maternity cases and was superseded in 1898 by a larger building.

The children's accommodation and school

This was finally added in 1886. *The Christchurch Times* decribed the new children's quarters as follows: 'Well-built, of a light and airy character ... well-appointed ... every convenience close at hand ... Not elaborately furnished, but furniture chiefly new. In the centre of the ground floor is a schoolroom, with the governess's apartments and kitchen adjoining. On either side of the building is a day room, a work room, a bathroom and a lavatory (fitted in the running-jet system that ten might wash at the same time). Upstairs, the rooms comprise of a sick room, clothing stores and bedrooms. The bedrooms are so arranged that each child has a separate bed. The girls and boys have separate but similar rooms, the boys occupying the suite of rooms on the eastern side, and the girls on the western side. There is a staircase on both sides. The present number of children in the House is 23 boys and 13 girls, but accommodation is provided for 60. The boys and girls each have a large playground which is divided by a wall, but they both enjoy an uninterrupted outlook toward the town. The children are isolated from the adults, only meeting in the dining hall at meals, their access to the House only being approached by a footpath to a door into a corridor near the able-bodied women's ward.'

I have quoted the passage almost in its entirety as it so well illustrates the classification system at work, the efforts to avoid the children coming into contact with the undesirable adult paupers, and the open aspect then surrounding the new buildings.

The children's accommodation was only in use for about ten years, after which it was converted to a female infirmary. In later years it was once again used by children when it became a children's hospital ward. Its most recent use was as a day hospital for the elderly.

The original lying-in ward.

This little building was added in 1898 as a new lying-in ward to replace the smaller one adjacent to the infirmary. The plan below shows space for ten maternity cases at any one time. The long corridor shown in the photo was added after the women's infirmary was moved to the empty children's accommodation, to which it was linked.

Other buildings on the site by the turn of the century included a huge laundry, much added to over the years, which used pauper labour, and the nurses' home at the corner of Fairmile and Jumpers Road. More of this later.

One of the first telephone systems was installed in 1886 between the Master's rooms and the school, and extended by 1889 to link up the lying-in ward and infirmary.

The Lying-in ward

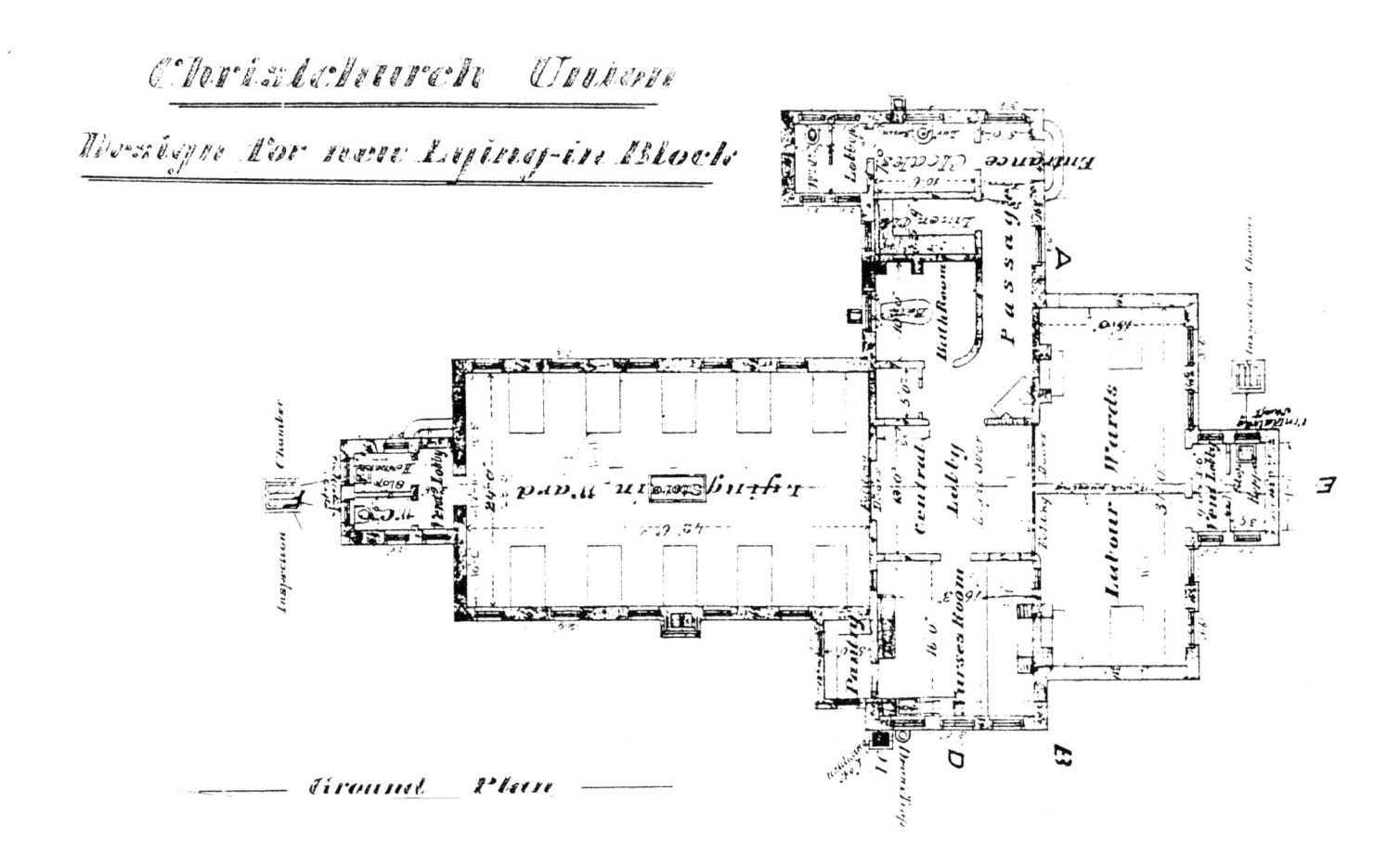

Christchurch Union
Designs for new Lying-in Block

Ground Plan

CHAPTER EIGHT

the new regime

The following poem appeared in *The Christchurch Times* in 1895:

The workhouse opens wide its door
And says to all 'Come in!
I welcome both the sick and poor
And those worn out with sin.

'Come in, thy gentle blear-eyed sot
(For though no liquor's here),
You'll find it warm and snug, I wot,
Till summer doth appear.

'Come in, ye girls that fallen are,
Ye shall have doctor's care,
And food and drink superior far
To honest women's fare.

'Come in, ye aged, poor and neat,
And live with those who swear,
You'll have the self-same food to eat,
And self-same clothes to wear.

'And when the ladies give their treat,
No difference shall be made
Between the vilest of the street
And the most virtuous maid.

'Ye working men, mark well my word
Ye neither drink nor play,
But, if ye keep the workhouse "bird",
The piper ye must pay.'

(attributed to 'Mellor')

In the first year of the new House, 1881, the 'vilest' and the 'virtuous' were entered alike into the Admission Book for that year and make interesting reading. They included hawkers, laundresses, shoemakers, painters, sawyers, plasterers and labourers, alongside a 'nurse' (not entirely a respected occupation then), and a 'sexton'. A bricklayer, washerwoman, widow, housemaid, cook, butler, charwoman, servant, dressmaker and a carpenter were also in the book. But one would not expect to find a musician, a photographer or a schoolmistress, although they were there. Perhaps it really was the demon drink that brought them to the workhouse door, as was so often claimed, though not entirely without justice, by certain Guardians in these avidly pro-temperance times.

A fine example of that breed of person so despised by the workhouse authorities, the so-called 'in-and-out' type, appears by the name of Charles Harvey Atkins. Mr Atkins was admitted no less than 29 times between November 1885 and October 1887, sometimes reappearing on the same day as his previous discharge. This name crops up again in 1896, when a man referred to as 'Atkins' was forceably ejected from the boardroom, having 'on many occasions wearied the Guardians with his petty grievances'. His particular offence was to have demanded of them whether they were 'Guardians of the poor or guardians of the Poor Law'. One cannot help but think it was the same man.

Other cases were plainly in the category of the virtuous: the deserted widow, the four children deserted by both parents, the two-year-old boy whose parents were in 'Winchester Gaol' and who was brought in by the police.

The fear of the workhouse by this time was very deep-seated. An inquest on an elderly man who had died just a few minutes after being admitted to the infirmary was told that, though he slept in a woodshed on Jumpers Common on a layer of straw, and suffered from heart disease and dropsy, he would only consent to being admitted when dying on being told it was a hospital and not a workhouse to which he was being taken. The Preface provides another example, of course; the reluctance in that case probably directly contributing to the child's death.

Life was indeed harsh inside. Not even old men were exempt from the requirement of work. Some of even 80 years of age had to chop wood: in 1898 the Guardians thoughtfully erected a wood-chopping shed for them in their yard. The able-bodied females were engaged as before in the laundry and housework, although it would be wrong to imagine that this would have been light work. It was far more likely to have involved hours on end on hands and knees scrubbing floors. The inmate who 'refused to work' in 1891 on account of suffering 'aches and pains' all over from scrubbing, was probably quite genuine. Nevertheless, her inability to carry out the work cost her seven days hard labour in prison. Even infirmary inmates had to work on oakum.

The able-bodied males, still the class the deterrence principle was chiefly devised for, were put on stone-breaking. They had to break seven hundredweight of Mendip stone between the hours of 7am and 3pm. Another task was oakum-picking. When the painful fingertips this caused was brought to the attention of the Guardians they refused to believe it was true. 'To some people any work produced a disagreeable sensation,' remarked one. This task was also assigned to vagrants and led to protests from a more humane Guardian, Mr Harvey, who described it as 'distasteful and offensive'. It was meant to be, of course. Each man had to pick four pounds a day. It was not humane, said Mr Harvey: 'They are human beings!' Such an outburst of compassion usually left the majority of Guardians unmoved, as it did on this occasion. One merely sarcastically suggested that perhaps the men should have a game of marbles or billiards instead - this from the self-same Rev. Pretyman whose heart had gone out to the children at Tuckton.

Those inmates who made themselves useful were, however, given due recognition, albeit in a small way. One very helpful inmate had saved the Board a good deal of money by doing odd jobs, and after much agonising about the correct response was rewarded with an extra ounce of tobacco each week. Conversely, the pages of the local paper are full of court cases of workhouse miscreants. Violence frequently broke out, and often involved the young women: one Annie Harris, aged 20, was lucky to get off with a caution for assaulting a fellow inmate. She threw water over her adversary and threatened to throttle her! In the young men's ward a notice had to be displayed forbidding 'blasphemous or obscene talk'. Some things never change . . .

There were other more desirable occupations included working in the garden. In the many acres owned by the workhouse, both potatoes and strawberries were grown. The strawberries were served up to the Guardians, but eventually they magnanimously forewent this little perk in favour of the inmates, at a later time when attitudes had softened.

The diet seemed to be reasonable. In fact, Christchurch Union was generous in comparison with other workhouses in Hampshire, supplying precisely 27.5oz of meat each week as opposed to 17.7oz elsewhere. Such exactitude reflects the almost legalistic approach to the dietary rations then adopted. The water, which was drawn from wells, left much to be desired, being found by Dr Hartford, the Medical Officer, to be 'very bad indeed' in 1891, containing swarms of organisms. Whilst that particular well was put out of use, it was not until 1896 that mains water was used by the workhouse. Lunatics were still kept at the House, and no proper provision ever seems to have been made for them. Reference to padded restraints and to the Western Counties Idiot Asylum at Starcross, Exeter, are made, so, as before, some were sent away and some stayed. Alcoholics were included in this category. Other ill inmates had the benefit of the infirmary, in which the medicinal use of alcohol was very common, and led to queries from the Guardians about the quantities consumed. In 1898 they had noticed that the quarterly consumption of brandy had risen in only 15 months from one gallon to 15 gallons! Although the Medical Officer was expected to find the money for medicines out of his own pocket, brandy was the exception and the ratepayers footed this bill! Dr Hartford did point out that some unions sent their incurable patients away, but Christchurch did not, and brandy was then an important stimulant.

A clue to the workhouse uniform is provided by a reference in the local newspaper in 1898 to blue serge being adopted for male infirmary patients instead of corduroy.

Numbers in the House had soon risen to a level where the buildings were quite full - over 200 in 1897. When this information was revealed in the local paper's usual reports of the board meetings, a helpful reader wrote with a kind offer to take an eligible woman off the Union's hands! His request for a wife was rejected, but gave the Guardians much amusement. They even suggested sending the man a sample. Perhaps the applicant had the last laugh, as he subsequently received over 200 offers of marriage in reply.

The question of classification still obsessed the Guardians, and in 1896 they turned their collective mind to further refinements of the divisions between classes of inmate. The following is the scheme that was subsequently introduced:

The 'Infirm' classification was sub-divided into two groups -

A(1) Men over 60 with 10 years' residence in Christchurch without having claimed poor relief, unable through no fault of their own to maintain themselves;

A(2) Men over 16 temporarily 'infirm' and of previous good character with residential qualifications as above; also

A(3) Widows with children, deserted wives with children, with character and residence qualifications as above.

This 'A' group was permitted privileges such as permission to walk in the gardens, frequent leave of absence, a separate table in the dining hall and better clothing (woollen suits) with no distinction or uniformity of character. Their sleeping arrangements were upgraded and divided into personal cubicles, over 7' by nearly 3' in size. Small though this space appears, it was apparently able to contain an iron washstand, folding bed, a chair, a box, a small shelf and a mirror and was even carpeted. It was their task to keep their own cubicle tidy. The men were entitled to a tobacco allowance and the women to snuff. The class As were given a day room, also carpeted, with the luxury of armchairs, tables, shelves - and, the crowning glory of 'coloured tablecloths'! They were also entitled to a better diet, including 2oz tobacco each week and tea in the afternoon.

From this group were selected the workhouse inmate posts of messengers, gatemen and wardsmen.

Other classes were sub-divided into a 'B' group. These were inmates over 16 of good character who had a satisfactory reason for not being able to provide for themselves. The only alteration to the existing conditions for this group was that they were to wear old workhouse clothes, not new.

All other adult inmates were classed as 'C'. This group was to receive the full deterrence treatment. No privileges whatsoever; distinctive treatment in all respects; strict discipline; their existing diet was to be down-graded; and they had to wear a distinctive uniform 'of the oldest and worst description'. They were to be confined to their yards and had only limited leave of absence. All the most disagreeable work was to be assigned to this class and no beer or tobacco rations were given.

In a survey in that year, of the 89 inmates to be reclassified, 13 were in the top A.1 category, one in the A.2, none in the A.3, 42 in the B section, and 33 in the C. So it can be seen that most of the current inmates would have lost privileges and suffered worse conditions under the new scheme. Not unexpectedly, it was not met by a wave of enthusiasm on their part. One courageous objector even went as far as to write to the Guardians describing the class A cubicles as 'hoss-boxes'.

The workhouse children

The children had school to keep them occupied, although rather joylessly it would seem, from the observation in 1887 by Guardian Rev. Clutterbuck that though they had a 'fairly creditable' examination performance, they 'appeared somewhat deficient in animation'. It is another disturbing clue to their lack of happiness that some would frequently manage to run away. One ten-year-old achieved four or five such escapes and once got as far as Ringwood. The Guardians reprimanded him, but washed their hands of the punishment, which was left entirely to the Master and can only be imagined. It was probably the birch: two unruly boys received this correction for misbehaviour in the school. They were, it appeared, beyond the control of the schoolmistress, and the episode led directly to the decision in 1892 to send the children out to school, commencing with these and other difficult boys. Eight boys even absconded from the National School. This little group's complaints were reported in the paper: they complained of ill-treatment at the hands of the workhouse's industrial trainer. All this does not suggest that the children enjoyed any emotional security. Persistently difficult children could be sent to an Industrial School.

The Local Government Board inspector, Mr Baldwyn Fleming, was very critical of the standard of care that the children were receiving. He pointed out to the Guardians in 1891 that they were dirty, many had chilblains and skin diseases were common. The lavatories they had to use were unclean, and their beds were untidily made. It does not do the officials of that time much credit.

They were expected to take their fair share of work in addition to their schooling, which typically meant domestic chores for the girls and gardening for the boys. Some effort was made to alleviate their boredom, which the Guardians did by this time recognise as a legitimate problem, and from about 1897 balls and bats and skipping ropes were provided, especially through Guardian Mr Cooper-Dean; also books (though a Guardian objected to this as books were only thrown around, he claimed) and toys were obtained by appeal through the newspapers. Some kind and thoughtful citizens gave other items to fill their dull days with a little childish pleasure - a rocking horse or a picture book might come their way. It is sad to contemplate the lives of their predecessors without such frivolities.

Details of their diet survive and show that they had lunch at 10am, which was bread and dripping. Dinner was either bread and soup, bread and stew, pork and vegetables or beef and vegetables. On Saturday they were given boiled rice and jam. Like modern children, they did not care for the meat. Unlike modern children, this may have been because the pork came from the workhouse's own pigs, which were kept on fields on the other side of Fairmile.

The girls were still being trained for service, and in fact demand for them exceeded supply. Many boys went to Grimsby for work in the fishing trade, an 'apprenticeship' for which the Guardians paid the smack owners a premium of £5 even though this was a practice officially forbidden by the 1834 Act, and was extremely dubious as a destination for their charges. They were aware that stories were in circulation about the treatment received by the boys, and that those who wrote to the Guardians about their conditions would be only saying what the fishing-smack owners wished them to say. When Mr Cooper-Dean questioned fellow Board members about their suspicions, they owned up to having only followed up properly one of the many apprentices at Grimsby. The boys were indeed asked and consented to going into the trade, but Mr Cooper-Dean was probably quite correct when he pointed out that this was done because of romantic notions about life at sea gleaned from stories from the Bible. One Christchurch lad did become a captain of a steamer; another was returned as unsuitable, his romantic notions having been rudely dispelled. When actually asked what they wished to do, out of eight boys, one wished to be a telegrapher, one a soldier, one a gardener, four sailors and one ambitious little chap, 'nothing'. A life in the navy was indeed an alternative, many boys being sent to training ships at Southampton, and army life was also an option: more than one drummer boy originated from Christchurch Workhouse.

Provision for the littlest children was haphazard at first, until a nursery for them was established in 1895 to replace the prior arrangement of using 'the most respectable women in the wards' to mind them. Despite concern that such lavish care would encourage illegitimacy, a ward was sub-divided and a day attendant employed; at night the babies could return to their mothers if they had one. A couple of years later, six prams were obtained after a public appeal, and the days when the babies and toddlers were confined in one room all day came to an end.

The lives of the older children also improved as the century drew to a close. The Guardians then recognised that it was 'wrong for them to be shut away from the outside world through no fault of their own', and the great step forward of allowing them to go to school with ordinary children came in 1892. They were readily identifiable, all the same, until the distinctive workhouse garb (described by Guardian H. W. Jenkins as hideous) was dropped in 1895, before which the boys had to wear knickerbockers. Despite this, they still looked alike, as later pictures of them show. In the same year they began to attend Sunday school and church. Girls were given nightdresses to wear, and toothbrushes; all these seemingly minor improvements illustrate just how deprived of normal comforts the children had been up to then.

The children were still discriminated against by the authorities: in 1899 the National School demanded a fee for their attendance, something not required from ordinary town children, probably because the school was supported by voluntary contributions and sought to boost funds by billing the Guardians. No such defence can be made for the Congregational Day School in Millhams Street, whose schoolmistress, Miss Smedley, haughtily informed the Guardians that she had instructions not to admit Cottage Homes children. It will be seen later what opposition came from state schools.

A great experiment was conducted in 1892 which proved to be successful: the boarding out of children. At this stage, only orphans and abandoned children could be considered for this, not the ordinary poor, so they were in the minority, but undoubtedly a lucky one. At last, such children 'had something in the nature of a home,' said a Guardian. Foster parents were paid a fee of £5 a week - more than most other parents had to raise their children with, as the Guardians were acutely aware - and were conscientiously visited by the Ladies Visiting Committee on a regular basis.

Strange to say, this arrangement was finally to account for the care of almost all poor children by the end of this story, but was only in its infancy then. The biggest alteration in the conditions of the children who remained in the workhouse came in 1896 with the opening of the first of the 'Cottage Homes'.

The Cottage Homes

The rationale behind this development was the new concern to separate the children not only from the adults but from the workhouse itself, a decision that was made by the Board in 1892. A new morality was pervading the boardroom regarding those in its care who were blameless for their plight, and even though they recognised that their plans for separate homes for groups of about twenty children would cost more than having one large block, they desired 'to do what's right and best for the children'. 21 acres opposite the workhouse were acquired from one of the Druitts and four Homes and a schoolroom were built by W. J. Chinchin and were ready at last in February of 1896. The map below shows the layout, and the architect's plans their appearance. Each Home was approached by wrought iron entrance gates and pillars.

Overall responsibility for the Homes was in the hands of a Superintendant and Matron: the first appointed to these posts were Henry and Alice Dyer. The Guardians had argued vehemently for control to be vested in the workhouse master, but the Local Government Board would not permit this. Later developments at the Cottage Homes give rise to interesting speculation about how things might have turned out had the Guardians had their way. . .

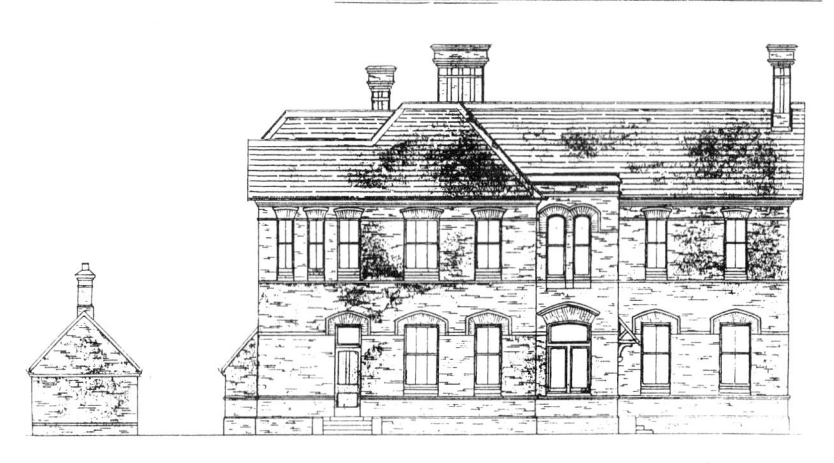

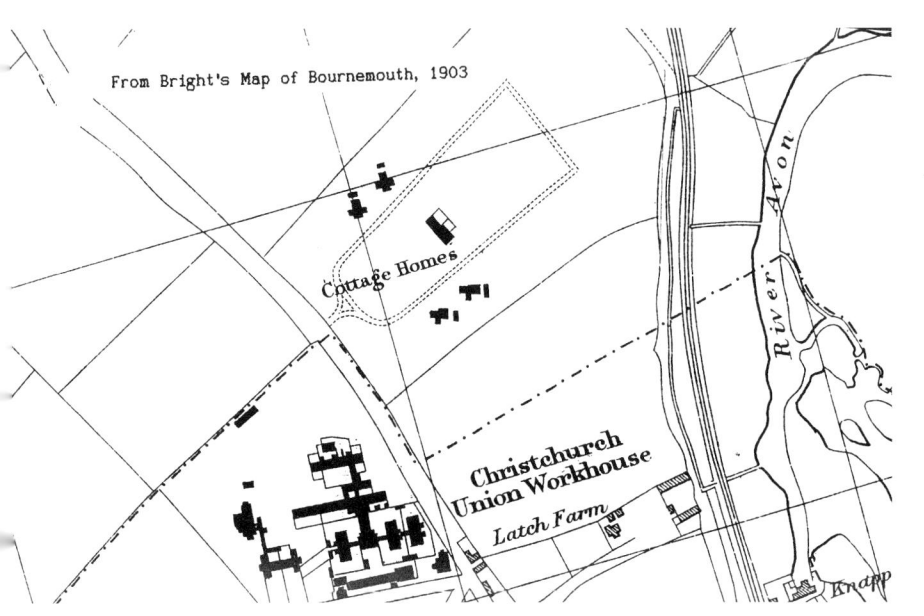

Each Home was run by an assistant matron and was surrounded by large plots (which the children cultivated) with a central green on which the school was situated. There were at this stage two Homes each for boys and girls, and those who had parents in the workhouse were allowed visits from them once a week, but were strictly forbidden to visit the workhouse over the road themselves. Swings and cricket balls were provided. Almost from the first day the new schoolroom was redundant as all the children went to the National School in the town (now the Priory School). The schoolmistress's services were dispensed with, but as the last school inspection revealed a 'great want of order', this was no loss. The assistant matrons taught the under-fives.

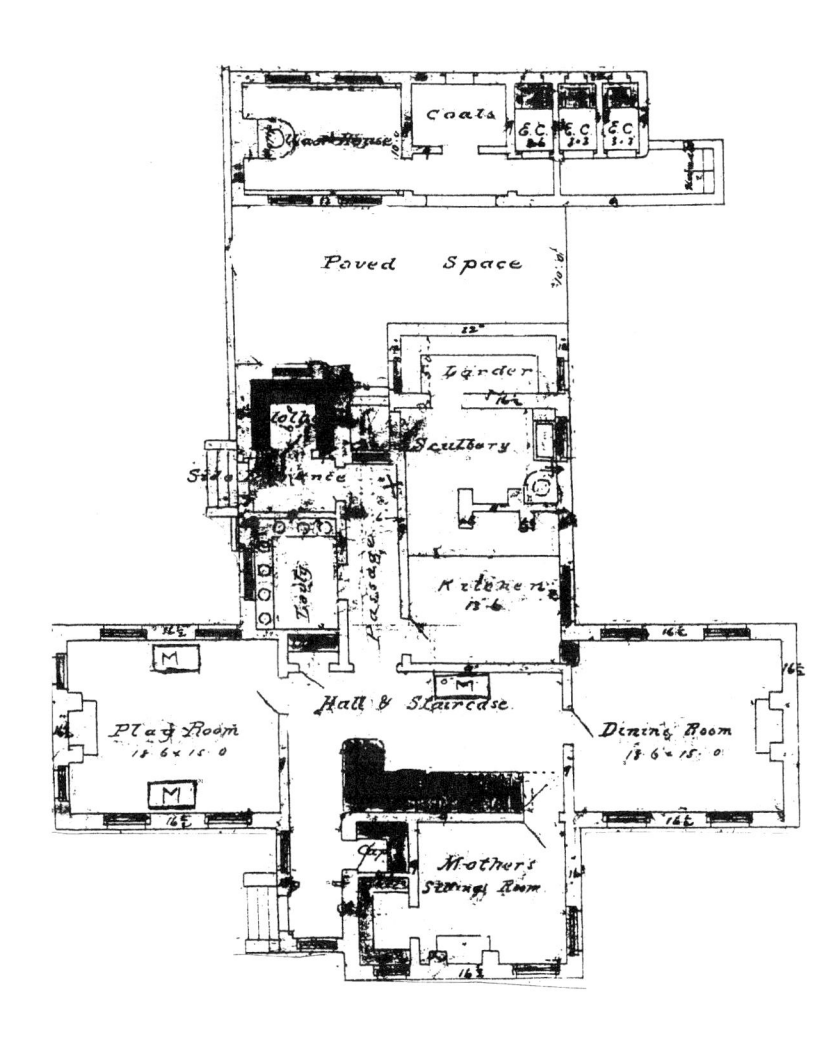

Ground floor plan of new Cottage Homes

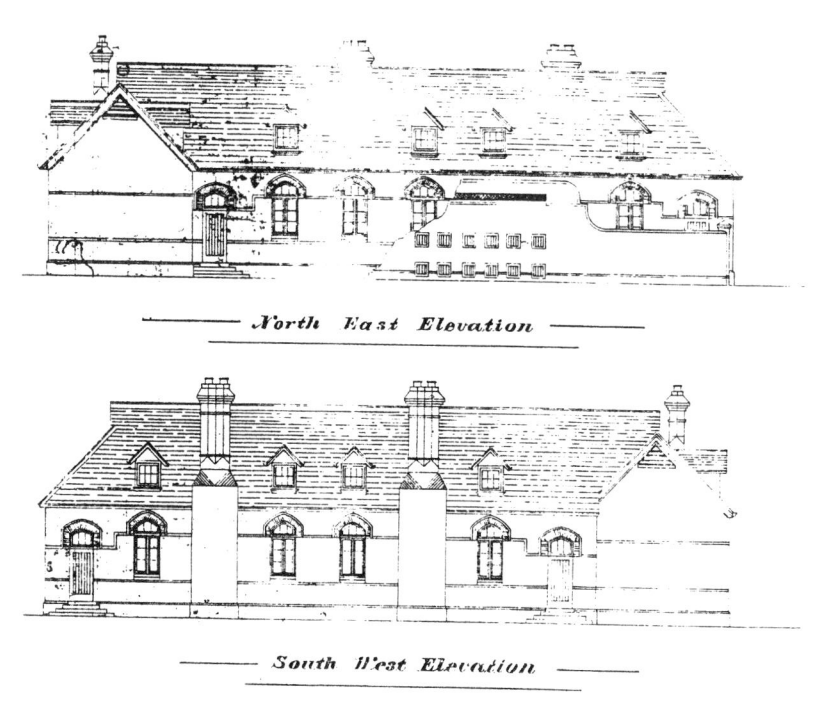

Christchurch Union Proposed New Schools

Life for inmates generally in this period continued to be enriched from tine to time courtesy of various public-spirited individuals and on special occasions such as the 1887 Silver Jubilee and the Diamond Jubilee ten years' later. Indeed, the frequency of such events was such as to cause concern to the Guardians, who always insisted that excursions to pantomimes etc were to be denied to the able-bodied. George Marshall (proprietor of *The Christchurch Times*) annually collected funds for the entertainment of inmates and maintained a list of subscribers which included Lord Malmesbury and some of the Guardians themselves. One

James Druitt (courtesy The Red House Museum)

year he was so incensed by the refusal to allow him to entertain the majority of inmates that he cancelled his concert. Always the Guardian most keen to make workhouse life unvaryingly tedious, it was James Druitt's insistence that the workhouse was not 'an assembly room for concert parties' that caused the difficulty.

One kind offer received an even more contemptuous rebuff and is worth recounting at length purely for its hilarity value:

It began just after the move to Fairmile, in mid-December 1881, and when the Guardians were at their most autocratic. A John Butler, of West End Farm (Castles ironmongers, today), wrote to the Board offering to perform some of Handel's Oratorio for the inmates on Christmas Day. The Board scoffed: the inmates 'were not quite up to Handel's music, and probably not up to who Handel was,' sneered one member.

Their rejection duly appeared in the next issue of *The Christchurch Times*, prompting an enraged Mr Butler to demand an apology. Instead of getting one, all he got was hearty laughter from the Guardians, although they did have the belated courtesy to reply in writing to his offer, with thanks.

The spurned would-be benefactor was having none of it and wrote two more letters to the Board, which the clerk 'would not trouble to read' and wrote to refuse to accept any further communication.

At this point, now March 1882, the writer seemed to become unhinged. 'The pen is mightier than the sword,' he dramatically wrote to the Board, and mysteriously rambled on about an eye for an eye, each man has his price, and other well-worn phrases. He concluded his diatribe by demanding £5 or an apology.

Later in March he somewhat recovered his composure, and apologised about seeking an apology, but insisted on the money being handed over. The letter was left to lie on the table, but not before it had been greeted by further contemptuous guffaws.

By April, the Guardians had ceased to see the funny side. The next letter, not revealed in the paper, had merely become 'tiresome'.

A long silence followed, after which their antagonist sent them best wishes for a happy new year. It was now 1883. More laughter.

April saw another communication from Mr Butler, this time of the unhinged variety. 'Gentlemen, I am a fool', he announced to them. The chairman remarked that the contents of the letter 'raised no controversy' and the Board 'unanimously agreed to the sentiments of the writer'.

The final letter from poor Mr Butler was allowed to remain 'on the table', its contents disappointingly undisclosed to *The Christchurch Times*. It was October 1883.

The vagrants increased dramatically once their unsalubrious new cells were opened at Fairmile, an 'ever-swelling and unsightly army of ne'er-do-wells' (*The Christchurch Times* editorial). They remained obstinately undeterred by the harshest of conditions, although they did get the benefit of heating after six chilly years, as it had been noticed that a hoar frost would form overnight on their blankets. Even when with an improvement in employment their numbers did decline, it was only remarked upon with withering scorn by the Guardians: Major Maunsell sneered that he supposed their treatment was not so good as formerly, and another raised a laugh by remarking that somehow no tramps came on Christmas Day.

Later, the same sarcasm would apply whenever the same situation arose - that Christchurch stone was too hard for them, for instance. There was never at any time any sympathy for their plight.

The workhouse had opened in 1881 with the Master and Matron, Mr and Mrs Saunderson, from the old workhouse. They could not have approved of the change, as before many months were out they had resigned, to be replaced by Mr Thomas and Mrs Martha Badcock, from the Woolwich Union. These two continued in their posts for only a few years, when they were replaced by Mr and Mrs Fey.

Guardians came and went: James Kemp-Welch died in 1887, and John Edward Holloway became chairman. On the Board in 1890 were Messrs Holloway, Maunsell, Lane, Harvey, Proudley, Sworn, Hoare, Jenkins, Moore, Beechey, Lander, Preston, Cooper-Dean, John Kemp-Welch and Aldridge. Many of these people served year after year without their election being contested. So time-wasting did annual elections become that they were replaced in that year by triennial ones. Ex-officio members for that year were Lord Malmesbury, Captain Elwes and Mr Eyre. These posts were abolished in 1894.

A major personnel problem that dogged the Guardians and for which they never found the solution to nor the cause of was the difficulty in obtaining and keeping nurses. Accommodation was a problem that was initially addressed by providing them with beds in the old children's quarters. Though a nurses' home was built at the corner of Fairmile and Jumpers Road in 1902, when there were only eight nurses, neither this facility nor any other made any difference. Various explanations were put forward: that Christchurch was too dull for them (so they were provided with a piano which on later enquiry the Guardians found none of them could play); it was too far for them to walk from the nurses' home to the infirmary (so they were provided with Ulster coats and spare uniforms); salary too low - it was increased; work too exhausting - ward maids provided. To no avail. A squabble with an inmate about the exact position of her leafless pot plant led to the huffy resignation of one Nurse Manser, who then wrote to *The Christchurch Times* complaining of the staff indiscipline and bickering, and went off to seek another occupation, 'tired of the Poor Law'. By 1904 a nurse was resigning at almost each Board meeting. It cannot have helped that the Board was so strict about them: all the outside doors of the workhouse were locked after 9pm, so even though the nurses complained about the effect this had on their social life, it was a regulation that was not lifted. Something had to be done: in 1913 it was decided that the workhouse should train their own nurses, but as we shall see, the problem continued into the era of the welfare state.

Bournemouth and Christchurch both grew rapidly; new wards and districts were constantly springing up. Some of them, e.g. Winton and Springbourne, housed the working people who were the main users of the workhouse. The committees spawned by the Board grew relentlessly: there was a Finance Committee, School Attendance Committee, Vaccination Committee, Assessment Committee (rates), Relief Committee, Workhouse Committee, Classification Committee, Ladies Visiting Committee and a Buildings Committee, all of which in the words of a 'Long-Suffering Ratepayer' writing to *The Christchurch Times*, 'vie with each other in adding expense to expense'. Even a Guardian, Mr Preston, was worried. Christchurch, he said, was 'constantly being told that it was the most expensive, most extravagant, yet best-kept workhouse in the country'.

This last smug comment was severely tested by a major scandal that hit the Guardians in 1890.

CHAPTER NINE

the public inquiry

In September 1890, a Nurse Sarah Ann Matkin wrote a courageous letter of complaint to one of the Guardians, Major Maunsell, and thereby set in train events that shook the Board out of its cosy complacency.

'Two lawyers and a couple of parsons, a number of builders and estate agents, a few farmers and a sprinkling of tradesmen, an officer and a couple of country squires, with one or two of the nondescript class called gentlemen, and you have our Board.' This withering assessment was made by a Guardian, the Rev. Cleale, under a pseudonym, in *The Christian Magazine*. Although it relates to 1896, the composition of the Board had hardly altered since The Great Scandal.

The nurse's complaint about the treatment of a patient, brought to her in the infirmary 'more in the manner of a dog than a human being', was of sufficient weight to postpone the funeral and order a coroner's inquest. The coroner ordered an investigation, news of which was printed in *The Christchurch Times* and *The Bournemouth Directory* and afterwards in *The Salisbury and Winchester Journal*. The scandal even reached the ears of the London reporters, who in *The London Star* referred to the 'simply shameful' situation of a 'poor old man dying in a workhouse without attention or food'. Newspapers loved workhouse scandals, of which there were many examples, the more lurid the better.

The gist of the accusations was that an inmate was admitted through illness but died after three days without having received medical attention or food. There are both heroes and villains in this story, but it is basically one of mistakes and mismanagement, rather than deliberate cruelty.

At the insistance of the Local Government Board, Mr Baldwyn Fleming came down from London to conduct the inquiry, which was very professionally handled and lasted three days. Many witnesses were called, both inmates and staff.

The inquiry heard that one John Campbell, a wheelwright-cum-carpenter of Christchurch, aged 60, had come to the workhouse on account of ill-health, and, therefore, presumably inability to work, on a Friday in September. He had seen the porter, Eli Troke, and had the usual bath, after which he was examined by the then Medical Officer, Dr Legate. The doctor gave him a very brief check-up, and directed him to the old men's ward. In fact, the man was suffering from heart disease and should have been sent straight to the infirmary, as the doctor must have known as he had checked his pulse.

It was observed by a witness that Campbell could barely put one foot in front of the other when he came into the ward.

Once left in the ward, Campbell's condition caused his fellow inmates serious concern: he was far too ill to get up to go to the dining hall for food, and the other inmates had too much fear of the officers and wardsmen to ask for help for him. Even a glass of water, which he had begged for, was refused by the porter, who told another inmate that only the Master could authorise such a request to be granted. Campbell was by the Sunday pleading for food, moaning, gasping, with cold hands and feet, blue lips and in great pain. He asked why it was that 'they should be so cruel to me; I have never had a shilling out of them all of my life.'

Campbell did get to the infirmary in the end - slung over the porter's back and carried in this manner down the stairs and through the long corridors. On reaching the infirmary at last, he died within ten minutes. Dr Legate issued a death certificate without having seen the body, giving cause of death as angina.

The negligence of the doctor is obvious. Had he given Campbell the attention his illness demanded he might have lived longer, or at least died with due care and attention.

Other workhouse officials plainly showed themselves in a most unfavourable light: the porter who was surly and rude and who Nurse Matkin accused of 'gross and wilful neglect'; the Master, Mr Fey, who should have toured the wards each night but did not; the schoolmistress and the industrial trainer who plainly lied about having seen Campbell in the dining hall eating his dinner; the Guardians who were not sure if they had the right to actually set foot in and inspect the workhouse that they were responsible for (in fact, only those Guardians actually serving on the Visiting Committee had this right), and in particular, James Druitt who tried to make out that Campbell had merely caught a cold on his final journey through the damp meadows - always the most eager apologist for the system.

The inspector, Mr Fleming, quite rightly ruled that those responsible for the scandal should pay the price. The Master, Mr Fey, was dismissed, along with the Matron and the porter. They had all been informed that Campbell was unable to leave his bed, but none of them had taken responsibility for attending to him.

Mr Fleming also demanded the dismissal of Dr Legate, who showed 'culpable carelessness' in the initial diagnosis of his patient and lack of instructions as to diet or treatment. Unbelievably, the Guardians strongly resisted this instruction, but were obliged to carry it out. Their protests did, however, result in Dr Legate being allowed to keep his post as the District Medical Officer, dealing with the recipients of out-relief.

Improvements were made as a result of this public examination of the failings of the workhouse. The Master and Matron were now obliged to attend at each meal in the dining hall and visit each inmate twice daily. The Visiting Committee inspected the House each week, and made surprise visits to the wards to question the inmates directly without the Master or Matron being present. The nurse in the infirmary was given a nurse assistant and was permitted to carry a supply of brandy as a stimulant instead of having to order it through the Medical Officer. The inmates got a clock in the wards and specific instructions about the use of the bell to summon help, which they had all been too afraid to use before.

From a staggering total of 74 applications, a new Master and Matron, Mr Harry and Mrs Laura Found, were appointed. A new porter and 'cook' (really, the porter's assistant, helping to wash the female vagrants) were also appointed at the same time. Not much later Mrs Found and the porter were each complaining to the Guardians about the other's rudeness, so it seemed that one rude porter was exchanged for another.

Mr Fey, whom the Guardians regarded as having been far too severely punished by the inspector, was selected as Vaccination Officer for the Union, the Guardians being genuinely concerned that he should not face ruin as a result of his dismissal.

As for the heroine, Nurse Matkin, she lasted two years before being invited to resign for the crime of playing cards with the inmates. She had brought to the attention of the Guardians not only this case, which she said was 'not the first', but other shortcomings such as underweight rations. But, such is the sweetness of revenge.

The inquiry proved of great interest in adding to knowledge about the routine in the workhouse. The inmates would file in to the dining hall (under the humbling inscription 'God Bless our Workhouse Master') for their meals. Breakfast was at 6.30am in summer, 7.30am in winter. Dinner, in the middle of the day, consisted of pork, potatoes and turnips. The bell for them to leave off work rang at 5pm; supper was at six. Grace was said before supper, everyone having to stand, before sitting down to a repast of precisely 6oz bread, $1^{3}/_{4}$. oz cheese, and a pint of tea. Each table was only allowed two mugs for however many people were sitting at it, so they had to share (until as a result of the inquiry they got a mug each). The bell rang again for bed at 8pm; the men had to put out the gas lamps themselves before retiring.

Inmates grumbled to each other about the stone-breaking, were loyal to each other - one who would not leave Campbell to attend the Sunday service was summoned for 'cheek' to Mrs Fey's office - and a crippled man had to be placed in with them in the aged men's ward because the young men taunted him.

From about this time, conditions in the House slowly improved. The bored old men were employed in an early form of occupational therapy known as the 'Brabazon scheme' by which they made baskets, rugs, wickerwork, woollen clothing and suchlike under the tutelage of the Ladies Visiting Committee, ably led and initiated by Mrs Risdon Sharp, wife of the prominent local solicitor. The committee was begun in 1895 and consisted of thirteen ladies who visited all the women and children. Their reports were initially treated by the Guardians with contempt; for instance, when they pointed out that the meat was too hard for the inmates to eat, the Guardians were greatly astonished and accused them of being too tender-hearted. Mrs Sharp was a force to be reckoned with, however. She was one of the first women Guardians and had a genuine interest in the poor, travelling miles from house to house on foot to visit the sick and infirm. She died in 1898.

The men in the Brabazon scheme received payment in kind, e.g. extra tobacco, and each year the results of their labours were sold in the boardroom to raise funds for new materials or provide extras for the wards, e.g. a gramophone. The women were not as fortunate: they 'had their full employ in other work'. This would most likely involve the laundry.

The old men got another perk in 1895: a smoking room. Elsewhere, smoking was banned, especially for the loathed able-bodied men. Some people showed that they could never be happy, no matter what - two men ended up in prison when they fought with each other because non-smokers were in the smokers' room. Today, it would be the other way round.

The old women got benches in their yards, and a supply of tea, milk and sugar to have the freedom of making a hot drink when they wanted one. Guards were put on the heaters in the wards for the poor laundry women who were attempting to dry their wet feet, and who had no other

The stained glass windows in the Inmates' Dining Hall, featuring a country lane, a sailing boat and a windmill.

footwear. Not that this modest variation in the policy of deterrence did not meet with howls of protest from some quarters. A correspondent, 'Christchurch Ratepayer', in *The Christchurch Times* bewailed this new liberality; 'It is pretty nigh time that the Guardians began to consider whether the luxuries and treats to the inmates of the workhouse had not gone nearly far enough . . . in addition to having well nigh a palace to live in, the Guardians are anxious to make the mode of life in the workhouse palatial also. The treatment of the inmates, children and all, is much more than coddling. It is feasting galore and housing luxurious! Why, **even Mr Druitt** [my emphasis] is suggesting slippers - not yet dressing-gowns for the poor overworked laundrywomen in the House.'

Times were moving on, however.

The appearance of the workhouse continued to change for the better. Mr Cooper-Dean generously donated 100 trees for the grounds in 1897, and the Guardians completed their last large building for the century - the lying-in ward (F Ward today), with beds for ten mothers. They built the corridor to connect it with the new female infirmary, converted the previous year from the children's accommodation. All was set for the workhouse to go into the twentieth century, but not without one last gasp from the die-hards. When Dr Hartford asked for fixed baths for the infirmary instead of the existing wheeled one, Mr Druitt was appalled: 'Fixed baths are a source of considerable danger,' he fulminated.

The new spirit abroad was ably expressed by a Guardian, the Rev. Cleale, writing, as previously mentioned, under a pseudonym in 1896:

'We call our board a progressive one . . . we keep pace with the times and we have the humanising tendencies of the day well represented. We treat our aged and sick as kindly as a Poor Law that badly needs reform will allow us. Our children go to the National School and can hardly be said to be clothed in uniform. Cottage Homes are in the course of erection. Non-Conformists and Roman Catholics hold a religious service in the House. A Ladies' Visiting Committee sees to a good deal that the Guardians would never observe. Our relief is fairly, judiciously given and when the Local Government Board sent down a circular recommending the classification of paupers according to character and conduct . . . we set to work at once.

'Of course, we differ very much . . . [There are] great distinctions between the old-school Guardians who are still wedded to the principles of the Poor Law Act of 1834, and the new humanitarian school. Not but what the old school members are humane enough in their own way - one of the most rigid is often ready enough with a little bit of help out of his own pocket to a case the Board cannot touch, but they act on a different principle.

'They are terribly afraid of making pauperism too attractive . . . Do away with uniforms? Why? They are paupers and you can't make them any other. Remove the children from the workhouse surroundings? Stuff and nonsense! The children have always turned out well . . .

'The old-school Guardians have a great dislike to paupers adding to their miserable pay by taking any kind of remunerative employment . . . [it] seems very hard that a widow with four or five children and not 10s a week to keep them, may not put a few things in her window, or let part of her house, or take in a little washing . . .

'It is hard to be a conscientious Guardian, to steer straight between inclination and duty, between the humanity that would deal tenderly and the mistaken kindness that encourages pauperism and sets a premium on vice. It is difficult to help the unfortunate without encouraging the idle.'

The aged had won some understanding and consideration; sympathy for the young pauper was far less forthcoming:

'. . . modern Poor Law administration made the House, for old folks, a kind of almshouse in which they might end their days in peace and comfort. The whole system of the Poor Law has changed since its beginning and changed for the better in regard to the aged and infirm. They [the Guardians] could make up for the increased comforts of the old people by being extra hard on the young,' Guardian Mr Whigham told a Board meeting to enthusiastic 'hear hear's.

With this ominous message to the young able-bodied, so many of whom were soon to perish in the bloodbaths of the Somme, the Guardians entered the new century.

CHAPTER TEN

the Edwardian era

The first building projects of the new century were the nurses' home, already referred to, and a new boardroom, needed for the accommodation of the ever-increasing number of Guardians. Its construction necessitated the demolition of the married quarters, but this was not entirely regretted by the Guardians as they were aware that some of the craftier old people were marrying in the workhouse solely to improve on their accommodation! The boardroom put a stop to that sort of nonsense. The Guardians could now enter the site through their own entrance from Jumpers Road (now blocked by a window, but set in an attractive brick arch). Guardian Mr Toop called the new boardroom 'scandalous . . . a wanton waste of money', but others were pleased as the old one got unpleasantly full of tobacco smoke.

The Board also discussed a new laundry to replace that in the row of workrooms between the dining hall and the infirmary (constructed in 1912) and further vagrants wards, which were eventually built, but their time was to be taken up for more than ten years by the question of a new infirmary, arguments for and against which dragged on all this time with delay after delay and frequent changes of mind.

The steady increase in the number of inmates was the principal reason for going ahead. Numbers kept on reaching new highs: 288 in 1908; nearly 300 in 1913. The principal cause of the postponement and indecision was the national legislation regarding the introduction of old age pensions, the effect of which would, it was felt, remove the need for further infirmary provision, and, in the ultimate scenario, lead to the abolition of the workhouse altogether. In fact, their concerns in this respect took many years to be realised, as the pensions were initially restricted to those who had not received poor relief during the previous twenty years.

The Nurses Home (from workhouse side)

The site for an infirmary was bought in 1905 from Lord Malmesbury, who sold the Guardians six acres adjacent to the existing buildings, a site graphically described by Mr Cooper-Dean as 'one of the most disagreeable and unsuitable in Hampshire. On one side the cemetery, on the other the mortuary, and in front, the sewerage farm.'

Political debate about the future of the Poor Law led to resolutions to defer the infirmary and then these resolutions would be rescinded at the next Board meeting. Small wonder that Mr Druitt lost all patience: 'It was a fact', he said, 'that at one meeting some five or six Guardians came and did the business, and the next another set came and reversed the business done at the former meeting, and the consequence was that there was no continuity of works.' Boardroom dissension even spilled over into the press, with chairman Mr Kemp-Welch and Mr A. J. Abbott conducting an argument in the correspondence columns of *The Christchurch Times*.

Meanwhile, the infirmaries were bursting at the seams, and people were having to be discharged prematurely. The infirmaries were 'more and more looked upon as a poor people's hospital,' observed the Master. The Medical Officer, Dr Batley, was most concerned that the overcrowding meant that ordinary patients had to be mixed in with lunatics, who shouted all night and must have been exceedingly irritating, to say the least, for the inmates, not to say frightening. This situation continued until the new laundry was built just before the first world war, and the 'lunatics' were housed in the old one.

At last matters came to a head with a visit from the very capable Local Government Board inspector, Mr Baldwyn Fleming. He was able to persuade the Guardians that they had a 'clear duty' to provide the extra infirmary accommodation, so desperately needed. Failure to do so might lead to the breaking away of Bournemouth as a separate Union, allowing other, poorer, parishes to join in with Christchurch. Although this advice was dismissed by Mr Toop as 'moonshine', Mr Baldwyn's sensible approach gave the Guardians the confidence to proceed. He had explained to them that their fears about the cost, estimated to be about £20,000, were immaterial: since the workhouse was built in 1881, when there was a population of 29,847, and the last figures available from 1901, when the population had reached 69,339, the cost of relief had decreased by $1/2$d per head. The infirmary would, in fact, add only $1/4$d to the rates. (Interestingly, it was shown in the discussions that total expenditure since the workhouse was inaugurated was £50,395.)

Baldwyn Fleming then retired, after many years of giving the Guardians much sound advice, and chiding where necessary. His successor was Mr John Walter Thompson.

In 1910 the architect, once again Mr Burton, was instructed and a tender for £8,641 was accepted from Jones and Seaward of Bournemouth, and the new infirmary, now H Block, was opened in January of 1913 by the wife of the chairman, Mrs Kemp-Welch, receiving this accolade from *The Christchurch Times*:

'. . . new, up to date, magnificent . . . Built of red brick and Victoria stone, roofed with Portmadoc slates, with floors of polished maple blocks and . . . wards heated with the latest pattern combustion stoves, and there is a complete installation of electric lighting. There is an excellent kitchen, lavatories etc, and the walls of the building are thoroughly distempered. The infirmary has two verandahs on the west side; one end points due south, and the rooms are devoted to tubercular disease. There are twelve wards, the largest of which on the ground floor is 98' long, and the two large ones upstairs 60' and 36' respectively. There are 86 beds, all fitted up in the latest and most comfortable style.'

Tea was served to 'eminent' visitors, and a 'sumptuous' tea laid on for the inmates, with apples, oranges and sweets distributed, followed by a concert in the dining hall.

The new male infirmary

With this lavish new provision for the men, the old infirmary (then also for men) became the quarters for aged women and married couples, with the little lying-in ward next to it a work room. As the new occupants were in the favoured aged category, the walls of the yard were reduced in height to 4' (obviously, yard walls must beforehand have been too high to have been able to see over), and topped with trellis work.

The following year, the name 'workhouse' was dropped, in favour of the alternative 'Fairmile House' as a concession to those born there who would otherwise bear a stigma, but not before another sarcastic reactionary Guardian had called out his own suggestion: 'How about Crockett's Hotel?' - a reference to the incumbant Master.

The shame of having to go into the workhouse went very deep. In 1902 a hero from the Crimean war by the memorable name of Cornelius Everett, was 'compelled' to end his days there by 'sheer want', reported *The Star*. No funds were available for naval men, and he had a horror of the workhouse. A man charged in 1913 with failing to maintain his children was ordered by the court to remove them from the workhouse, or go in himself. 'I don't want to go back to that horrible place,' he roundly declared, preferring to abandon his children and spend a month in prison. One elderly lady committed suicide rather than go into the workhouse infirmary. The separation of couples was still practised up to the outbreak of World War One, as shown by the complaint made by an inmate whose wife had just died in the workhouse. She had been sent, he said, into the young women's ward, which he described as an 'ice-well', pronounced fit for work (needlework), and died a month later of cirrhosis of the liver. He had not felt able to visit her, not even allowed to ask. To complain, he said, meant 'Winchester (prison) staring you in the face'.

Still, conditions steadily improved. Despite the typical resistance of Mr Druitt, another Guardian, Mr Nugent, purchased out of his own pocket a supply of newspapers. Mr Druitt was appalled: it was humbug, he said, to provide inmates with newspapers; they would be wanting other luxuries next. On some occasions, the Guardians clubbed together to assist a deserving applicant - in this way a one-legged hawker received the means to return to his native Yorkshire.

Diet got better; the bread was no longer rationed and tea was offered at breakfast as an alternative to cocoa. At one Christmas, so much food was on offer that one inmate died of excessive over-eating. This disclosure at the inquest so enraged a ratepayer that he wrote to ask how such a thing could happen, when in the country as a whole 100 people died of starvation each year - some of them receiving old age pensions.

The numbers of the able-bodied paupers was worrying, particularly young women who came in to the House several times to have a child but refused to give the clerk the name of the father, so that maintenance could not be obtained from him. Bournemouth seemed to have a bad reputation in this respect - the largest proportion of illegitimate births of all towns. Mr Cooper-Dean thought that the current enlarging of the laundry where such recalcitrant women had to work would 'put a stop to it', but it did not, and the nursery became very overcrowded. Eventually, the situation was eased by sending the little ones who were in the care of the workhouse over to the Cottage Homes at two years old instead of three.

Contemporary events are often referred to in the newspaper reports of Board meetings. An obstinate elderly woman who had been sleeping rough appeared before them in 1908. She refused to speak to the Board and was given notice to leave the workhouse. Mr Newman, a member of the Board, recommended that she joined the Suffragettes!

It was in this period that female emancipation was more directly experienced by the Guardians with the election of the first lady members in 1901. Mrs Risdon Sharp, who inaugurated the Brabazon scheme, and a Mrs Berry, joined, to be followed by Mrs Alice Shave and Mrs Grimes. It was their arrival that speeded up the humanising process far more than slow parliamentary reform. It was Mrs Grimes's resolution that out-relief was to be paid for children (in 1908) and who acidly commented that this 'had only one defect, and that was because it was proposed by a woman'; Mrs Grimes who publicised in the press the case of a 'beautiful boy' in the workhouse nursery who needed adoption; and Mrs Grimes who led the way to the Board doing whatever it had within its powers to do to alleviate unemployment. She also had a ready answer to the male Guardians who thought that she could not be their equal: when her membership of the

Buildings Committee was queried, in that she might not know anything about foundations, she defended her abilities and then quietly added: 'besides, I have served twenty years' apprenticeship to an architect as his wife'. Latter-day feminists will also relish her comment to her male colleagues regarding three men who went into police custody for not performing their tasks: 'Then the men are not **all** good!'

Mrs Shave was also a determined and caring lady. She arranged for the Cottage Homes children to get a donkey and cart for outings, and organised the appeal for one herself, despite the usual sarcasm from other Guardians -'how about a motor car?' . . . 'or a liveried servant?', they quipped. She understood the needs of children who would have to leave the close confines of the Homes without a friend in the world outside and arranged for them to make return visits. Her influence was felt to be so powerful in the boardroom that when she was absent on account of her husband's illness, Board member Mr Abbott said that it did not feel like a meeting of the Guardians without her.

These ladies must certainly have blown much-needed fresh air through the boardroom. Mr Toop was still a Guardian at 88 years old after 30 years on the Board. He retired at that age but was co-opted a few weeks later back on the Board! He died the following year, 1913. John Kemp-Welch was also a Board member in excess of 28 years by that year.

The Master and Matron for many years from 1898 were a Mr and Mrs Alfred Crockett ('splendid officials' said Guardian Mr Nethercote, 'the most valuable servants the Board has ever had.'); by 1905 there were 34 officials, including the clerk, five medical officers, a chaplain, superintendant matron at the Cottage Homes, assistant matrons and nurses.

Christchurch Union.

Union Workhouse.

A. CROCKETT.
MASTER.

Christchurch.

As for the casuals, their numbers were also still on the up. The town mains water scheme of 1904 and the tramway works the following year brought many into the town in quest of work. A survey of 1904 showed that their numbers had increased dramatically in twenty years, from a total of 37 in 1884 to a total of 308 in that year. The majority were aged 30-40, closely followed by the 60-70 age group and the 50-60s. Most were men; there were a few children. These were sometimes dragged around by a vagabond parent to boost their funds through the sympathy they elicited.

In the casual wards the men were having to sleep two to a cell. There was a brief labour shortage at the time, but Mr Crockett told the Guardians that the casuals were outcasts that no one would employ. Their diet remained dull and inadequate - bread and cheese if they remained all day on task work, dry bread if not. The same hard work was exacted: 14cwt of hard stone or one ton of soft stone each day. They were not exactly made to feel welcome. Only the prospect of being arrested for 'sleeping out in the open without visible means of support' for which offence they could expect 7 days' hard labour, could have obliged them to seek shelter here. They persisted with the traditional tramp protest of tearing up their clothes, and continued to receive the usual response from the authorities of a prison sentence. Occasionally, a more violent protest was recorded, such as by a man who broke down his cell door. 'Prison is much better than the workhouse wards,' he shouted, probably entirely justified, as he was led away from court to commence fourteen days hard labour. Sometimes, tramps simply ran off: this incurred the risk of appearing in front of the magistrates wearing clothes which were the property of the Guardians to the value of 25s.

Both the casuals and the able-bodied were also put to work on the workhouse land, which amounted to some 12 acres in 1899. A horse and cart were purchased at this time to assist the cultivation. Typically, the purchase of an account book soon followed in which to keep a careful record of the work it was doing over on the Cottage Homes fields. Not much seems to have been achieved except the waste of ink, as the farm was described in 1910 as being in a disgraceful state. There were no able-bodied men to work it, and those who could be found seemed to have no idea - one man told to weed the marrows chopped them off instead (or was this a rebellious protest?).

With the advent of the new Insurance Act in 1912, at least those in possession of such insurance were excused the stone-breaking. The stone, incidentally, came from Shepton Mallet at a cost of 7s 2d a ton, and was sold after breaking to the Christchurch Rural District Council for 7s 11d a ton.

A hilarious misfortune befell a lady in 1904. She cannot have been very well-dressed, as although she was only a visitor, she was mistaken for a new inmate and plunged into a bath used nightly by vagrants. This 'brutal outrage', she said, had 'ruined her for life.' She was all of 76 years old.

The children at the Cottage Homes were sometimes said to be better off than outside children,, even according to the local education committee. A Guardian from Dudley Union was 'astonished to find such luxurious places provided for poor children'.

They had the donkey cart, through the efforts of Mrs Shave, and were given drill instruction for an hour every Saturday in the empty schoolroom. This was later kitted out as a gym, with hanging rings, Indian clubs, dumbbells, parallel bars, and mattresses made by workhouse labour. There were outings every year paid for by the Board to such places as Chewton Glen, and other distractions, such as tea and sports with the mayor. A Scouts troup was formed in 1911, and only two years' later they won 1st prize at the Hampshire Scout Camp at Netley, to where they had marched 15 miles, there and back.

The Blakeboroughs came to the Cottage Homes as Superintendant and Matron in 1901 and quickly made an impact on the Guardians who saw them as 'capable, efficient and painstaking'. A house was built for them in 1902, by Jenkins and Son at a cost of £1020, and a store adjoining for £582. The Homes themselves were filled to capacity and over, more than 100 children was not unusual. Because of this, it was decided to construct two more Homes, one each for boys and girls, but the outbreak of war was to delay this.

Christchurch Union.

R. BLAKEBOROUGH
SUPERINTENDENT

Cottage Homes,
Christchurch,

19..11..1921

The Blakeboroughs stopped the children from running all over the road and going into the little thatched cottages that then lined Fairmile Road on the way to school in the town; now they walked neatly in procession. These times are now in living memory, and the sight of the Cottage Homes children being marched to school is well-remembered, as were the Blakeboroughs, who were, in fact, a grim and intimidating pair, very strict.

South Elevation

The Superintendant's House

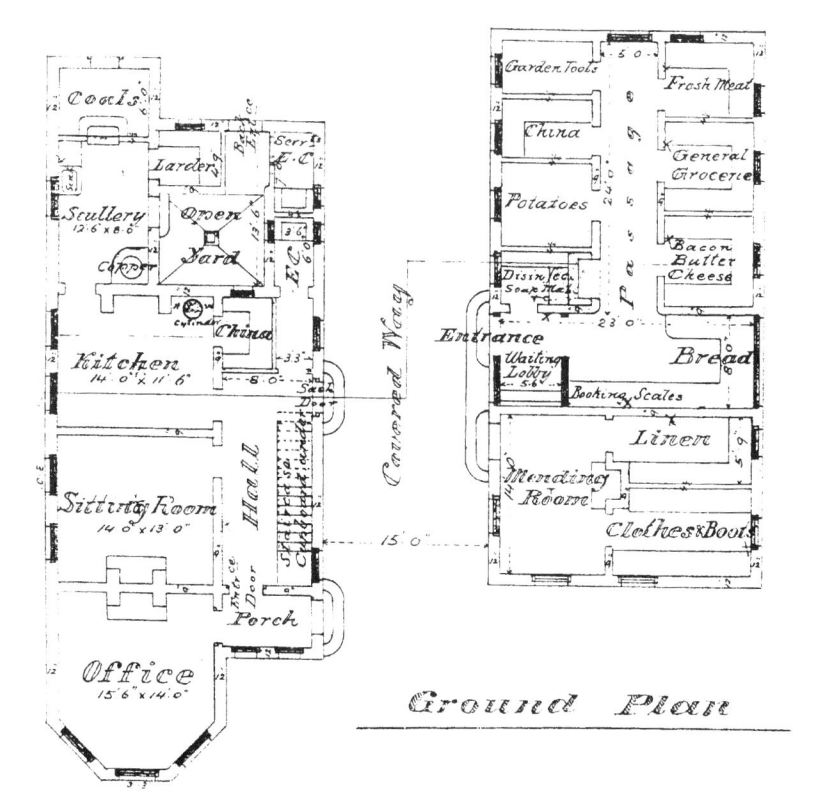

Destinations after the Homes remained the same - for boys, the army or navy, or apprenticeships, and the girls went into service. A new prospect was available for boys from 1910: emigration to Canada to live with families and work on their farmsteads.

The fishing trade was another outlet. In 1913 an ex-Cottage Home lad who had joined a Brixham fleet five years before saved the life of a fellow apprentice. The Guardians were extremely impressed and decided to recommend him to The Royal Humane Society. Although this could not proceed, the Guardians decided to make their own award to him, and presented him at The Cottage Homes with a silver watch and chain, medal and Bible. 'A fine speciman of a young Englishman', *The Christchurch Times* called him. His name was William Tiller.

Those boys who found other apprenticeships were considered by the Guardians to have opportunities that were not available to many other children, but the chance they were given did not always prove to be to their advantage. A Boscombe bootmaker would not give the Guardians their premium back when his apprentice absconded. The poor boy was badly overworked, his hours being from 8am to 1pm, then 2pm until 5pm, and then again from 5.30pm until 9pm. He was beaten and his wages were not paid. This was in 1911; he was 18. Alan Druitt argued that the boy was not overworked, but the case was found against the bootmaker - not for mistreatment but for failure to fulfil the conditions of the apprenticeship.

This sorry tale was matched by the typical life of a girl in service. In 1908, the Minutes of the Cottage Homes Visiting Committee recorded one aged 14 learning to make baskets and chairseats and to keep the house tidy. She was up at 6am, began work at 7am, so had to last two hours before breakfast at 8am. She then worked from 9am until 1pm; 2pm until 5pm, then, after tea from 6pm tp 6.30. Even then she was not finished, as she then read to her employer until 8pm, before going to bed at 9pm. This child described herself as 'happy and contented'.

A little girl of just four years old was a new arrival at the Cottage Homes in 1911, and still has vivid memories of her first encounter with the matron, Mrs Blakeborough. On account of her mother's illness, her father had to bring her and her little sisters to the Homes; they walked the five miles from Winton. On her way, the child picked the flowers from the hedgerow as a bouquet to present to her 'hostess' on arrival. Mrs Blakeborough remained unimpressed by this childish gesture of affection, and disposed of the bunch in the nearest waste bin, before the child's astonished eyes. She was then ordered to strip and put on the workhouse garb - this under the curious and very public gaze of fellow inmates.

The Cottage Homes children at school.

Other aspects of life in the Homes are just as vividly brought to her mind, over eighty years later. Overcrowding was so bad that the children had to sleep two to a bed, nose to tail. Breakfast was porridge - only without either milk or sugar; by the time she reached school she and her companions were already so hungry that they would fight over scraps of food discarded by the road. Tea was a thick slice of bread, with either margarine or jam - not both, together with a mug of cocoa. By the time she left the Homes, she was a 'proper skeleton'.

That aside, there was no physical maltreatment in those days. The children were frequently visited by adults seeking a child to adopt, a procedure apparently without formalities: someone would arrive, pick a child, and leave with him or her. One titled lady selected this little girl's sister on one such visit. On being informed that the child was not available, the lady offered £2,000 - £3,000 to her father for her. This was an enormous sum of money in those days, but her father refused it.

For one and all in the workhouse Christmas was the occasion for indulgence and relief from the daily grind. They were able to enjoy not only the traditional Christmas dinner, with beer donated by Lord Malmesbury, but extra treats such as a carol service at the Priory, a lantern slide show or other various entertainments - a conjuror, a ventriloquist, a musical concert. The beer question was debated *ad nauseum* in the boardroom each and every Christmas for about 25 years, always the subject of a resolution from Mrs Grimes, a fanatical temperance campaigner, and one who remained utterly convinced that most of the inmates could blame their woes on drink, and always she was defeated, usually heavily.

The children at the Cottage Homes had a Christmas tree from Lord Malmesbury, with gifts for each child underneath, prizes and toys.

Every year Rev. Bush would invite the adults over 60 to tea at the vicarage in spring: 1903 was the twentieth year in which he did so. There were other special occasions that the inmates could participate in: in 1902 it was the Coronation. Not all the Guardians took the same view of such indulgences: One, Mr Hutchings, wanted to give the inmates a piano concert and hire a piano. After Mr Druitt again objected to the inmates receiving a little of life's pleasure, Mr Hutchings generously went ahead with his plans, paying for it himself.

Annual frivolities such as this came to a sudden halt in 1914 with the outbreak of the first world war.

CHAPTER ELEVEN

war

No sooner did it seem that hostilities commenced, then the Army arrived to assess Christchurch Workhouse for pressing into service as a military hospital.

The inspection in October 1914 proved satisfactory, and the following month witnessed the arrival of wounded Belgians to fill some of the 50 beds placed at their disposal in the old (original) infirmary. So began the vital and honourable role of the Red Cross Hospital in Christchurch which continued for the duration of the war.

All the staff with the exception of a night nurse were voluntary recruits - the 'VAD' (Voluntary Aid Department) nurses, from two detachments - 196 and 38 - under the efficient control of two lady 'Commandants', Miss Louden, of Hengistbury House, Christchurch, and Miss Ricardo, of Bure Homage, Mudeford. These two valiant ladies immediately drew up a list of wants and energetically set about acquiring them. On the list, which was published regularly in *The Christchurch Times*, were pneumonia jackets, flannel bandages, blankets, cakes, cigarettes (Woodbines were especially appreciated; it seems incredible today that smoking was positively encouraged), soups, jellies, poultry and so on, a miscellaneous list that could include almost anything. A special band of lady egg collectors was even set up. Details of gifts received as a result of the appeals also went in the paper.

The Red Cross made many alterations to the infirmary to adapt it to its new use. They put in a larger kitchen range and installed gas heaters in the wards for hot water. There was also an operating room. New wards were added, utilising buildings that the Guardians had used for other

(Courtesy Red House Museum)

59

purposes, increasing the hospital's capacity to 80 beds. These opened in October 1915, 'spacious and lofty buildings of wood and corrugated iron, with brickwork chimneys', reported *The Christchurch Times*. Each of the two wards was 66' by 25', lit by electricity, with bathrooms and lavatories attached. They were christened 'the South Africa' and 'New Zealand' wards. Names of the Empire were used for all the wards at the time - others were Malta, French etc. Also there was a Kitchener and a Haig ward.

Soon afterwards, a strange addition was also grafted on - a boathouse lent by one Mrs Scott, which was used as a recreation room. New appeals went out to equip it with furniture and games.

The Commandants had under their direction various Medical Officers, 40 Red Cross nurses, Quarter-Masters, a housekeeper (Mrs A. Druitt), four cooks and ten kitchen helpers. A stretcher 'company' was based at 15 High Street, now the Library, under the command of Major Gardner, with a Mr Lord second-in-command.

The Guardians felt the loss of the old infirmary accommodation keenly, but got it back in its extended state in January 1917 - having been obliged to hand over their larger and brand new infirmary to the Red Cross, so great was the need. The men were being sent from the trenches by sea to Southampton and from there by train to Christchurch, where they were met by volunteer 'ambulance' drivers who brought them to the hospital. Such was the continued need that by April, the Guardians were faced with a request from the HQ of Southern Command to hand over the entire workhouse for the sick and injured soldiers. They did not do so, but a year further on handed back the old infirmary to the Red Cross. Where the inmates were moved to is not recorded, but it is probable that out-relief was more generally given. Both infirmaries were then Red Cross hospitals. The Red Cross had begun their work at Christchurch with 50 wounded soldiers; by the time the Armistice was signed they had 300.

Whilst this account provides the bare bones of these events, a moving insight into the work that was done by Christchurch people to aid the soldier-victims of the battlefields has been left to us, a tribute that provides a remarkable record of one who was on the receiving end of the marvellous work that was done here. Some anonymous but gifted writer sent a series of articles to *The Christchurch Times* in 1918. I make no apologies for including the lengthy extract that follows.

A HOSPITAL TRIBUTE

We Come to Christchurch
By "Malta"

The twin screws wildly thrashed the water for a moment or two, we heard the scraping rattle of the anchor chain sliding out, and then Chippy said quietly from the next bed, 'Thank Gawd, that's Bloighty'. As the boat's bow came round, the sun shot a column of light through the one porthole by which he could peep in - 'Jerry's' malevolence had closed the rest - and used the dancing waves as reflectors to make his welcome more evident still. And we were soon to see him, for the orderlies quickly hoisted us up from the ward to the deck. There, in the clean sunshine and clean, bracing air with its sea tang, we had our first sight of England as we lay in ordered rows on the stretchers awaiting our transference to the train. Beneath the cloud-flecked sky, the wheeling gulls screamed their welcome, the honest whistle of a passing engine shrilled to the same key, and the strong sea wind whispered it to us as we lay there silently, joyfully, expectant. And it was with this chorus of welcome that Blighty began the cure of her sons broken in the wars.

The quick, competent, nonchalant orderlies soon switched us off the boat and onto a stretcher carriage into the ambulance train, where the padre was waiting to take air wires to the home folk, to distribute stamped postcards, or to obtain newspapers, whilst in the shed was a girl waiting to do her bit with a supply of sweets and a very obvious willingness to do any old job for us, from the posting of letters onwards. And as we lay waiting for the train to start we wondered idly ... whether these offices of welcome would continue for long, whether we should leave them all behind us at the port.

A whistle from the engine, and we began to glide along an English railway and see English placards, and be stared at by English eyes set in English faces; but our destination was still on the laps of the gods ... Then came a very smart, button-polished, chin-shaven sargeant, who passed along from stretcher to stretcher with the detachment of a professional providence and informed us all whither we were bound. 'Umpteen, you're for Christchurch,' was the remark he tossed to me. But it left me cold, for Christchurch was nothing but a name, its excellencies were still to be found, and it needs but a very short military experience to rob one of all sense of responsibility ... Soon, the engine began to slow down, and curiosity was awakened as to Christchurch; what sort of a place it was, how we were to be treated, was food strictly rationed, and were the hospital rules reasonable. As the train stopped, we saw on the platform civilians, armed with stretchers and with a look of nervous anticipation on their faces; we did not know that they were real *amateurs*, lovers of their work. The 'walking cases' were soon out of the train and off to the hospital, whilst we 'more unfortunates' were left in helpless, curious uncertainty. In came the first two stretcher-bearers and were directed to their patient 'number so-and-so', but their nervousness was still as evident as their willingness ... the nervousness was lest by any kind of awkwardness we might be caused an unnecessary twinge of pain. The bearers could not realise that we should have thanked them if they had caught us by the legs and arms and dropped us on the stretchers, for how can those at home know what Blighty is, and all that it means to us? And we too did not at first realise what it was to shed our numbers and become men whose need was tenderness, gentleness and utter kindness. Orderlies would have unloaded us with the swift, heartless efficiency we knew so well, but we were receiving the treatment accorded to sick friends who had come home. And all the little nervous mistakes only made us more certain we had come back too, and deepened our consciousness of the atmosphere of absolute kindliness that pervaded the whole platform.

... Cigarettes came in a shower, and those, too, of the right sort ... Were we smoking, then it would soon be finished, and if we hadn't one, the want must be immediately supplied. The slightest draught stealing gently through the door produced an extra blanket, and the need of a match meant the gift of a box. We had shed our numbers and become honoured guests, treated with the lavish hospitality that comes naturally from the right kind of Englishman, a type surely indigenous in hospital.

Our welcome had exceeded all our anticipations; in its kindly forethought, it almost transcended our belief, but gave us an assurance that while we had been 'over the water', those left behind us had neither forgotten nor forsaken us.

We Arrive at the Hospital

'Well, boys, you are awfully lucky to get to Christchurch,' remarked one stretcher-bearer as we 'more unfortunates' lay helpless on our orderly stretchers in the waiting room. We made no response, but puffed away stolidly on our cigarettes ... But Christchurch as yet was nothing but a 'place' ... It had been pointed out to us on a map, and it was merely a little round black dot with a name tagged on it ... Consequently, all remarks about the place fell upon uninterested ears. We were in 'Blighty', and that was as far as we could comprehend.

It was a 'Blighty' sky we could see through the windows, English men were running around, intelligible advertisements hung on the walls; 'Blighty' was about us everywhere, so how could we feel interested in Christchurch? . . . Therefore, no enthusiasm was aroused. The Christchurch hospital might be 'the best in the South of England,' but we know that a little actual experience was worth a considerable deal of puffery. 'It's a V.A.D. hospital, you know.' That admittedly was worth knowing. 'The building's quite new, too,' added another, and then, as an afterthought, 'and it's run entirely by ladies'. We thought we might quite like Christchurch, an opinion that was confirmed by a gentleman by the door who remarked with unction and appreciation, 'Yes, boys, and they're all pretty. There are men who bear you to hospital, and bore you when they get you there, They smother those apparently in Christchurch, none come to maturity.'. . . The time had at last come for us to be loaded up, and up we went to the top storey of the ambulance and started off. But the spring had got into the veins of that driver, the exhilaration that can only come with the feeling that one is doing good, had fevered her blood, so quickly he switched us off out the station, shot us over the bridge, whisked along Fairmile, and sent our hearts into our mouths with the turn into the hospital, jerking them safely back again as she drew up at the door. With a strong steady pull, we emerged from the ambulance hood, were carried past the polished doors with their immaculate brass, and set down in the entrance hall. Why is it that the entrance halls of all hospitals bid you to abandon hope? . . . There was a bareness, a chill, a loneliness about that hall that depressed us . . .

'Malta' was the ward to which we were assigned, and up the stairs we went, 'specials', as it were on the landing to guard us and ensure our safe ascent. But on reaching our destination a feeling of great and final contentment was ours . . . We looked round about, and everywhere the blatant efficiency characteristic of the military hospital was camouflaged, swamped, hidden beneath that dainty lure of colour which is the distinctive note of the right kind of woman. The chill, white, patternless counterpanes of the military hospital were gone, and in their places a bright-patterned pink, spotlessly, but not obtrusively, clean, and the screen too did not stand up in utter nakedness, but their white wooden frames were draped with the same pink fabric that hid the untidiness of many of the lockers, and there were flowers too: some daffodils nodded their golden trumpets to one, whilst from the other side stole the delicate fragrance of the wild violet. In short, wherever one's eye lighted were obvious signs of the deft dainty hands of our womenfolk who have no peers the wide world over. But the last few words of an article are not sufficient to devote to our nurses.

An Inside View

. . . In the morning light . . . you become more sure of things. For in the cold, clear light of the dawn you see things as they are, and then you know it was no dream but a glorious reality. You actually feel sure that you are Home, that the nurses are real and substantial, that 'bully biscuits' are not on the menu, that we are in hospital, in a V.A.D. hospital, where there are neither early 'revallys' nor absurd or ridiculous rules. Then you turn over, prepared thoroughly to make the most of your good luck . . .

At the head of the whole hospital are the two Commandants, and only one of these two is known to us in 'Malta'. Now, the 'Commandant' suggests a grim, austere, bespectacled madam who says to this one 'Go' and he goeth, glad of the chance, and another 'Come' and shiveringly beneath her cold stern eye he cometh, and to another 'Do this', and he hops quick and doeth it tout-de-guile. That notion is the very antithesis, her spirit informs it, the men's utter contentment is the best testimonial to her efforts... And the Sisters in their sphere are like unto the Commandants. They listen to our tale of woe yet never look bored, nay, rather interested in the whole thing. At first it seems a bit strange to have a Sister who greets you with a smile and encourages you with a joke, is obviously interested in some jape you are tempted to retail for her benefit...And what can one say of the Nurses? That they are beyond all compare? But that of course goes without saying. One hears of the Waacs and the Wrens and the Land Girls breeched and legginged, their photographs are the mainstays of the Pictorial Press, but in the quiet wards of the hospital of the land girls are doing work about which there is no glamour, and around which the limelight never plays. But that does not mean that is unappreciated. We who gain by their work will never forget. The war will become a memory, the hospital a photograph, and Christchurch lapse again into a black dot with a tag on it, but the kindnesses of which we have been the recipients have been so indelibly impressed on our minds that they can never 'pass into nothingness'. And the great glory of the place is that the spirit is so widespread. It is no wise confined to this or that nurse, but is common to all. In fact, the only contention that one can imagine between the nurses is as to which of them shall show the greatest kindness and consideration to the patients temporarily in their charge...

The consequences of the war for the Guardians went far beyond the loss of the two infirmaries. The call-up meant that the dreaded able-bodied young men were very thin on the ground. We may expect the Guardians to have been delighted, but in fact they depended on workhouse labour to maintain the premises, especially their extensive grounds. The 28-30 acres were by then 'practically useless'. The Guardians considered this difficulty, and then came up with their usual answer - a committee.

Whatever the committee's solution was, it plainly did not work, as the War Agricultural Committee severely criticised the Board for the state of the land. The ground has indeed been sown, but the crops were lost through subsequent neglect, and this was in 1917, a time of acute food shortages. By the middle of 1918 the Guardians were seeking assistance with the cultivation from soldiers at Christchurch Barracks.

Rations were reduced in 1917 and the waste of bread was to be treated as a breach of discipline. The average weekly consumption of meat was 1lb per head, and of bread, 6lbs per head. On two days each week a pint of oatmeal (gruel) was substituted for 4oz of bread, though some inmates refused to eat it. Sugar was also in extremely short supply.

By April that year, the Government asked for the bread ration to be halved and substituted by flaked maize and oatmeal.

The casuals who swamped the wards each weekend (their numbers also swelled by the closure of casual wards at Lymington, Poole, Ringwood and Lyndhurst) were an especial problem, in that the physical work they were required to do used up excess bread supplies. They had a pint of oatmeal for breakfast and 8oz of bread with 2oz of cheese at dinner; by the following year they had to manage on precisely half this quantity of bread and cheese. The general workhouse diet in that year, 1918, was gravely inadequate. All that was provided in the infirmary seemed to be a thin slice of bread at breakfast, a herring for dinner and porridge for tea - the patients lay awake all night with hunger. The Guardians discussed this: Mr Crawshaw made the extraordinary assertion that he would welcome some of the substitutes himself, but they did agree to add 2oz of bread to the tea and breakfast. The Master could not get suet for puddings;

The South African Ward, Christmas 1915 (Courtesy of the Red House Museum)

boiled rice was substituted. He had plenty of sprats, he said, but no oil to fry them in. In the end, there was not even any cheese for the casuals.

The herrings on offer left much to be desired: a supply had been obtained that had been intended for export to Germany before the outbreak of war four years previously. German POWs had refused to eat them. A Guardian, Mr Baker, relayed the story to the Board and exhibited a sample, holding it aloft amidst much laughter. They were, he said, fit only for manure. Not all thought so: a Mr Beaton claimed to have tried them himself and found them 'very good to eat'. The proposition to destroy them was defeated.

In other respects, workhouse life went on as before. Christmas 1915 was celebrated as usual: 'The large dining hall at Fairmile House on Christmas Day', said *The Christchurch Times*, 'certainly did not give those present the idea of a seething mass of discontented humanity.' There was roast pork and beef, cabbage, potatoes, plum pudding, mineral waters and coffee, tobacco and snuff, apples and oranges. The soldiers had their own festivities, including competitions for the best decorated ward. Kitchener won in 1916, with an elaborate ceiling design of falling snow devised from the cotton wool supplies (obviously not rationed!).

'Seething discontent' was nevertheless as evident amongst the casuals - the majority of whom were described by the Master as old and decrepit men - as ever. One woman ran away in workhouse clothing and was given six weeks hard labour. A man who had worked in the morning on his allotted task refused to scrub the kitchen floor after dinner, saying it was three men's work. It may well have been. He was half-starved, he said, and could get no employment. No sympathy was given by the court. Colonel Brander told him there was plenty of work for able-bodied men like him, and sentenced him to a month's hard labour.

The Cottage Homes were a fertile recruiting ground for the army and navy, of course: almost 50% of the boys joined up on leaving and news of their progress was relayed to the Board meetings. There were times of sadness when the news was bad, but also times for pride when one did well for himself. A welcome letter arrived from an ex-Cottage Homes boy, now a man, who had joined up 18 years before as a drummer boy and had climbed the ranks to Sargeant-Major. He had, he said, 'fond recollections of Mr Found and also of Mr Macklin, his schoolteacher'.

Those whose destiny lay in a life at sea also kept in touch. One reassured the Guardians that press reports of unkind treatment on the training ships were incorrect. Only about one in every 200 men got flogged each week!

At the Homes themselves, then under the strict Blakeborough regime, the Cottage Homes Visiting Committee minutes suggest continuing unhappiness for some children. A girl of twelve ran away after being, she alleged, victimised by the matron of her home: her mother was insulted in her presence and the matron told her that she 'would sooner kick her out . . . than have her there', and she was often sent to bed after a supper of bread and water as a punishment. Her mother complained to the Committee, who heard from this matron, Miss Stagg, that the girl was a bad influence who fought with other children. The outcome was that the child was moved to another Home where she had a sister and away from that particular matron, who does not appear to have been cut out for the job of caring for emotionally disturbed children. The following year, 1918, two girls absconded because their hair was cut short on account of ringworm - a frequent problem at the Homes - and five boys later also ran away. The birch was used for punishment, but in this case the culprits were sent away to an Industrial School. Miss Stagg was again accused of physical mistreatment by other girls in 1919; this time she was warned by the Visiting Committee that they would not overlook further episodes.

When the war finally petered out in November 1918, the Guardians put on record their appreciation of the dedicated services provided by the Red Cross hospital. And got their infirmaries back, disinfected and cleaned.

Mrs Louden received the OBE for her Red Cross work during the war. She became President of the local Red Cross Society which operated from her home at Hengistbury House, loaning medical equipment to the poor. A Red Cross ambulance was begun in 1931, and the Society worked to raise awareness in hygiene, sanitation, infant welfare and tuberculosis. She died in 1939, just as a new European war was breaking out.

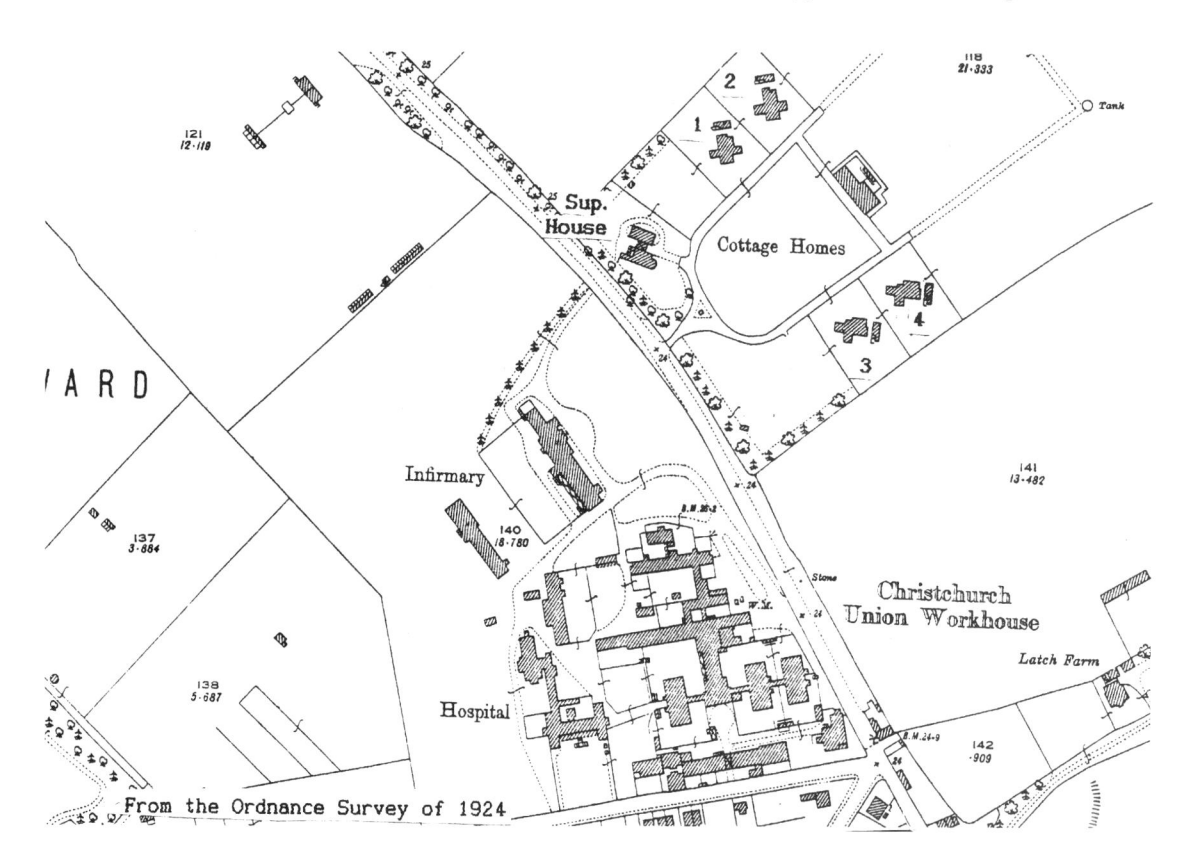

From the Ordnance Survey of 1924

G Block under Construction, 1924 – see facing page

CHAPTER TWELVE

on to the next war

The end of the first world war found the Guardians extremely busy making up for lost time. So much had had to be deferred, on account of the Red Cross, the price and unavailability of building materials, the shortage of labour and so on. Projects that had had to wait included the two extra Cottage Homes, the mortuary and the tramps' wards. These were to go ahead, but the first new building was to be an extension to the Nurses' Home which was completed around 1923 and filled most of the area between the existing home and the boardroom. (A further extension in 1933 joined the two buildings up.)

Then there was to be a new infirmary for the women. This was completed by 1924 on land to the rear of the site, and is now known as G Block. The open-air shelters were added in 1925.

The Womens' Infirmary in 1957, showing the glass corridor since demolished.

Almost as soon as it was built, the infirmary was taxed to its utmost, reflecting the slowly increasing medical, rather than economic, role of the workhouse. The entire block was therefore extended to the south to house another 44 beds in 1929. The work was done by the firm of Bryant and Trowbridge at a cost of £13,500, and the top floor was reserved for maternity cases. The Master, Mr Morgan, spoke of this achievement in his half-yearly report in 1930: 'undoubtedly one of the best of its kind in the country. Bright, cheerful and comfortable; its balcony will prove a splendid acquisition in fine weather, he reported. He went on to reveal that three side wards on the middle floor would be used as nurses' bedrooms pending the future extension of the nurses' home. The shelters, which are largely still intact, were used for TB cases. TB was rife through the 19th and 20th centuries until its spread was halted by the development of antibiotics in the 1950s, and it was common practice to keep patients in outdoor shelters all the year round.

Another long-delayed project was a new mortuary. This was built in 1928, and replaced one that had to make way for the new women's infirmary.

In the same year the tramp' wards (as the casuals were now more generally known as) were extended at a cost of £3,211. A new humanity was being demonstrated in their design; the cell system was done away with in favour of 'rooms resembling miniature hospital wards, lighted by airy glass skylights above', reported *The Christchurch Times*. The brick walls were with plaster, central heating was installed, a drying room for their clothes, three baths and a water spray, washing sinks and even a day of the Poor'. These are the semi-circular single-storey projections on the Fairmile Road side of the original infirmary.

The flurry of building work was also necessitated by the continually rapid growth of Bournemouth. The population of the Union had reached 104,068 in 1925, 90% of them residing in Bournemouth. The overwhelming preponderance of Bournemouth inmates forced a name change on the Board. From that year, it was known as The Bournemouth and Christchurch Board of Guardians. The relative positioning of the two towns' names was fiercely resisted by the Christchurch members: it must have been painful to accept that Christchurch's little Holdenhurst offshoot

The Mortuary

room for their food rations: 'The minimum necessary for cleanliness and comfort which they have a right to expect from a Christianised society', commented the paper. Such sentiments were echoed by Mrs Shave in her election address in 1928: 'Much of late has been done to give more light, air and colour to our buildings and to impart a greater aspect of warmth and cheerfulness to the whole institution.'

Such care and consideration were obviously appreciated: one Elizabeth Wood of Ferndale, Walpole Road, Bournemouth, left a sum of £2,000 in her will in 1926 to provide day rooms for those aged women 'whose circumstances and age necessitate the care and attention of the Guardians

The Elizabeth Wood rest rooms.

had grown so sturdy it was in danger of strangling its parent. The old Board's seal was acquired by Herbert Druitt, perhaps for his Red House collection. It would be most interesting to find out what happened to it.

This period saw the last of many Guardians that had been serving the Board for considerable chunks of their lives. John Kemp-Welch had given 45 years, 21 of them as chairman; Mr Kitcher 30 years, also chairman for many years; Mrs Grimes, now also a JP, had been 27 years on the Board by 1927. Another long-serving lady member, Mrs Dorset Shave, died in 1932. Her obituary in *The Christchurch Times* referred to the 'steady fire of perpetual kindness' she showed whilst undertaking her 'gracious work of inestimable worth'. Typically, she left provision in her will for income to be paid to the poor and needy on a regular basis. She was, incidentally, the aunt who brought up Mr Ken Smith, the well-known Christchurch church organist and ex-mayor.

A new broom was sweeping through the boardroom, and it was being pushed hardest by Bournemouth Guardian Mr Peaty, who was a very new sort of animal - the red-hot socialist. He claimed to be the only representative of the poor on the Board, although his assertion received this sniffy comment in *The Christchurch Times* editorial: 'From our experience [the Guardians'] primary duty has always been to relieve the necessitious poor'. But Mr Peaty was the genuine article. The traditional beer-for-Christmas debate received short shrift from him: 'It was not', he said, 'beer which was to blame so much for bringing about the downfall of men and women, but it was the environment of the latter which led them to abuse it. They did not hear all these tirades against the wealthy class when they indulged in intoxicants.' The beer had been donated for the occasion by Mr W. Hale, a Guardian.

By 1926 the number of nurses had risen to 26, and to 33 by 1930, although resignations remained a problem. A Medical Officer, Dr Lyster, suggested rather provocatively that some of them found conditions intolerable.

Mr Blandford, the Relieving Officer for the last 37 years, retired in 1926. It was estimated that in that time he had covered 60,000 miles in the course of his work. By bicycle. His replacement was Mr A. H. Smart.

Another change at the workhouse was the arrival of a new Master and Matron, Mr and Mrs William Morgan. 'He came to Christchurch in 1920 with a great reputation', said a Guardian, Mr Tunnard, 'which he has maintained ever since he was appointed.' One of his first initiatives was to plant trees along the Fairmile Road frontage. Mr Morgan became President of the Hampshire branch of The National Association of Poor Law Officers and was also an examiner for the Poor Law Examinations Board.

During the twenties and thirties, the porter and his wife were one Mr and Mrs Esterling. They brought their daughter, Charlotte, to live with them at the porter's lodge, and this lady, now (1994) 87 years old, is able to remember these days with great clarity. The late Master and Matron, Mr and Mrs Crockett, whilst kind enough in their own way, she recalls, were constrained by the Guardians from making any unnecessary expenditure. They were, therefore, unable to improve the lot of the inmates, whose standard of living was very basic.

The arrival of Mr and Mrs Morgan made a vast difference in this respect, as they managed to add the hitherto unheard of luxuries of jam and cake and milk to the spartan diet of bread and margarine. Mrs Esterling was particularly compassionate in her role of assistant Matron and then cook. Charlotte remembers how her mother would take advantage of the Master's absence at the sailing club to rustle up extra supplies of cakes for the inmates.

There was still a workhouse uniform for the women - grey dresses and a white apron and cap. It was, apparently, most unattractive, but the new Master did away with it and allowed the female inmates to wear pretty coloured dresses - still made in the workhouse, but much less of a 'pauper's' outfit. One day per month was permitted as leave of absence, for which occasion the inmates were given their own clothes back. The innate goodness of some of the workhouse officials is demonstrated by Mrs

Esterling's habit of giving such inmates half-a-crown out of her own pocket for their lunch,. One of the nursing staff, one Lucy Jefferson, was made from the same mould. She was Superintendant Nurse for some thirty years. The picture, kindly loaned by Mrs Charlotte Luckham, shows a rare photograph of the workhouse era. In the centre foreground are Mrs and Mr Esterling; behind them are some of the male inmates. They are making rice pudding in the kitchen.

More changes were afoot in the wider local government area: the ancient post of Overseer of the Poor, initiated 355 years before, was abolished in 1927. Although their function recently had been reduced to preparing assessment lists and collecting rates, their previous functions had included the burial of the dead thrown up by the sea, the issue of beer-house licences, prosecuting rogues and vagabonds, prosecuting those failing to maintain their dependents, prosecuting those who kept 'disorderly houses', preparing jury lists, and – of course, the relief of the poor.

In fact, the overseers were the earliest form of local government, out of which the Guardians had evolved. They in turn were now facing extinction.

But the Bournemouth and Christchurch Guardians had no intention of making a quiet exit after an existence of nigh on 100 years. The Poor Law was not being reformed, they said, just transferred to the new body, the Public Assistance Board. The transfer would be costly and the change was a result of 'a craze for centralisation'. Nationally, the same concern was being voiced by the Poor Law Unions Association, whose President's final address condemned the 'closing down of such a large body of voluntary effort' as ' a spiritual loss to the nation' and 'a national catastrophe".

One of the failings of the system was that the new pensions for the elderly and widows were inadequate, and relief was still needed. In 1925, there were 187 people over the age of 70 in the Union on relief; the majority, 100, were in the House. Three years further on, the new Old Age (Contributory) Pensions Act was passed, allowing those over 65 to receive the pension, yet only three people out of 156 then in receipt of poor relief came off it as a a result. Record numbers of people continued to be admitted; nationally in 1913 the Poor Law institutions and hospitals housed more inmates than in 1900, despite the pensions and 'the Minister's statement that these institutions are emptying', said the clerk. The increase in the old-age pension to 10s a week was simply insufficient to maintain them.

The Boards of Guardians were to be abolished on 31 March 1930. Agreement was reached on the management of Fairmile House. Christchurch was hived off from Bournemouth, so the long link going right back to the formation of the Union in 1834 was severed. Instead, Christchurch was to come under the jurisdiction of Hampshire County Council. Local people were most concerned that their relatives would not be allowed use of the infirmaries, but would be compelled to travel to Ringwood or Fordingbridge, but a stay of execution in this respect of five years was given. The Christchurch people were, of course, in a small minority by then. Figures show that on average in recent years only 55 locals were in Fairmile House and only ten in the Cottage Homes, all the rest being residents of Bournemouth.

It was thus The County Borough of Bournemouth which was awarded 'custody' as it were, in this tug of love.

The Bournemouth County Council created a Public Assistance Committee and a Guardians' Committee, the function of which was to advise the Public Assistance Committee on relief matters. Members of these committees included Cllr Gelsthorpe, Mr Kitcher and Mrs Grimes. In a valedictory article, *The Christchurch Times* applauded the Board with the following tribute: 'Fairmile House has earned for itself a splendid reputation . . .the best-equipped institution of its kind in the country . . . The Guardians have shown kind and humane consideration . . . for the poor and infirm . . . excellent work in the relief of suffering . . . Many of them have their heart in it so much that they are truly sorry for the change.'

The kitchen c.1920, note the kitchen cat.

There was one Guardian slightly sceptical. Mr Peaty's response to all this adulation was that 'he could not help feeling that evidence should be given by the men who had been in the wards and could give facts relating to the difficulties they were up against.'

The number of inmates had risen to 441 in 1926, partly on account of the General Strike. The good reputation of Fairmile House was widely appreciated by would-be inmates from outside the area 'trying to wangle their way in' (Public Assistance Committee, 1933) which was prevented by the Settlement Acts still being enforced. Incredibly, people appeared to be killing themselves because they could not get in, as opposed to the situation earlier when one person committed suicide rather than have to go in. In 1937 a man of 80 who had sold his cottage and was all ready to go into Fairmile House, did, unfortunately, actually do away with himself when he learned he was to be sent to Fordingbridge instead.

Those who did benefit from the care they received in the infirmaries would sometimes thank the authorities. One such patient wrote that it was 'more comfortable there than in expensive sanatoria'; another said that, 'I should feel condemned If I did not put on record all the kindness that has been shown to me at Fairmile House. I went there 14 weeks ago in an almost dying condition. Besides all the skilled attention, there were the little kindnesses, and the wireless added to my happiness and kept me in touch with the outside world.' This was installed in 1928, the funds having been raised by public subscription and the balance made up by Captain H. B. Norton.

Christmas was still celebrated in style, the inmates 'for a few hours living again as though the world had treated them fairly' (*The Christchurch Times*, 1932). Christmas in 1927 saw the nurses carrying lanterns through the wards and singing carols at midnight. That year the Priory choir visited the wards and parts of the House. In 1926 100 inmates were taken on an outing to the New Forest in a 'Royal Blue' charabanc; one old lady, taken there in a private car, had not been outside Fairmile House for seven years. Mrs Charlotte Luckham recalls that preparations for Christmas began weeks in advance, when the decorations for all the wards were made.

Unemployment in the twenties was high, and the Guardians attempted from 1920 to alleviate it when they could by giving the building work to unemployed men. Some worked on excavating the site for the women's infirmary, others were employed in the ornamental grounds and gardens, perhaps on the tennis courts that were laid out next to the new infirmary.

New consideration was given to the 'lunatics', now more kindly referred to as mental patients. Knowle County Asylum was still used, also the Park Prewett Mental Home in Basingstoke. As with all categories of inmate, their numbers increased, despite the passing of the Mental Deficiency Act in 1913 which was meant to relieve the Guardians of this responsibility. In 1920, three such people were maintained by Fairmile House in such institutions; eight years later the figure was 18. Still, a report from the mental hospitals was encouraging: no more strait jackets and their own cinema and concerts, with cricket and football for the men.

The veil of time preventing us from peering inside the House was partially lifted in 1927 through an article written 'by one who has been there' and published in *The Christchurch Times*:

'It is questionable if 90% of the pedestrians and others who daily pass the Poor Law imstitution ever permit themselves to wonder . . . how the inmates spend their lives. By a good many people a pauper is regarded with feelings akin to repulsion rather than a subject for commiseration . . .

'Some years ago, the Board of Guardians throughout the country, in an effort to remove the stigma of pauperism, abolished the term "workhouse" and substituted a more euphonious name for their respective asylums. True, a distasteful appellation has fallen into disuse, but -

"You may break, you may shatter the vase if you will,

But the scent of the roses will hang round it still."

. . . 'The institution under notice is commodious, scrupulously clean and distinctly hygienic in every way. Mr William E. Morgan is the competent head of the establishment, and his efforts for the welfare and comfort of

Rear of 'H' Block with corridor linking it to 'G' Block.

those under his supervision are ably seconded by the Matron (Mrs Morgan) and other officers, whose popularity, created by their untiring anxiety for the well-being of those under their care, is as genuine as it is general . . .

'The food [the inmates] are supplied with is wholesome, and not a few able-bodied men, and women too, could emulate "Oliver Twist". But when one considers that the work they have to perform daily (those who are capable of undertaking any) could not by any stretch of the imagination be styled arduous - in reality it is only exercise - the diet is quite ample.

'What hurts the bulk of the inmates . . . is the confinement. True, they are allowed certain liberty and their relatives and friends are permitted to visit them weekly, yet the privilege of freedom . . . is curtailed, and this rankles in most of them.

'Even some of the old men, particularly during the summer months, take their discharge periodically in order to feel that the shackles of restraint no longer bind them . . . On the other hand, there are some inmates who very rarely, if ever, go outside the walls, and this habit breeds a very uneven, cantankerous temperament, and as often as not they are soon ostracised by their former chums.

'The effects produced by an environment associated with a workhouse cannot honestly be said . . . to be conducive to health, especially during the summer months when the inmates are prevented from rambling through the grounds and enjoying the fresh air . . .

'Moreover, to not a few of the inmates the penned-up process is distinctly detrimental to their well-being. With some of them, melancholia [depression] is engendered and, try as they may, they are incapable of shaking it off, and eventually become anything but normal. Then tempers of others becomes deranged, irritability forming one of the conspicuous phases of their character.

'Some of the men and women are sub-normal when admitted to the House, while others develop strong mannerisms as a sequel to constant worry . . . Continually, one sees faces which suggest fretfulness, a sullen revolt against life and circumstances and fate . . . To the inmates who had decent jobs prior to the Great War and now find themselves cooped up in this fashion, the position is, to say the least of it, certainly nerve-racking.

'Of the inmates at present in the institution there is a good percentage of able-bodied men who ought, in the ordinary course of events, to be working hard at some useful occupation outside; while on the other hand, there are incapacitated old men . . . who are simply awaiting the arrival of the Grim Reaper.

'The majority of the men lead an empty, uneventful life, and although the soul-degrading restrictions and humiliations of the bad old days are practically evils of the past (the Poor Law system having greatly changed for the better. . .), there is still room for improvement with regard to liberty, the innovation of more useful work for the inmates, and reading facilities. Under the circumstances, however, the general body of inmates ought to be thankful . . . that such an institution is in existence.

'Notwithstanding the fact that the Poor Law is an admirable one, there are several distressing features about it. For instance, when a man leaves a Union institution . . . he is in exactly the same predicament as he was in when he entered the House - 'broke' financially, still without a situation and . . . shabbily attired . . . To turn a man adrift without money, in poor clothes, and with no employment to go to, certainly retards rather than facilitates his restart in life.'

This suggests that the dreadful tasks of stone-breaking and oakum picking may have come to an end during this period, something confirmed by Mrs Luckham's memories, as she could not recall any such work being done in her time. Then, women worked in the laundry and men, including vagrants, in the garden and on the land. Crops were then grown in the extensive ground behind the Cottage Homes and on the workhouse land in the region of the present-day MacMillan Unit.

The article also illustrates the lack of employment despite Labour Exchanges having been set up in 1909.

The Laundry c. 1930s, the inmates wear flowery pinnies; the staff in white.

The Laundry – the ironing room, note the gas irons.

The numbers of tramps using the casual wards during the inter-war period escalated dramatically and led to a headline in *The Christchurch Times*: 'Nearly 10,000 Tramps a Year!' in 1930. The article went on to chart the increase, which had soared from 952 in 1920 to 9,544 in the last year - a tenfold increase. The conditions remained unappealing: a visitor in 1926 was 'distressed to see so many men herded together and wished something could be done to give them more freedom on Sundays'. The Master pointed out that he was bound by the Casual Order of 1925 in the conditions in which the tramps were kept.

Their diet at this time consisted of a breakfast of a pint of tea with 8oz bread and an ounce of margarine. Dinner was 8oz of bread again, an ounce of margarine, 2oz cheese and some potatoes. Supper was as breakfast. This was the diet laid down by the Ministry of Health; there was never any meat, much to the concern of Guardian Mr Peaty.

By 1938, meat was appearing on the 'menu' for casuals, but a seaman who complained that it was tainted and discoloured and therefore threw it away, was punished with 14 days in prison for the offence, even though the Master had acknowledged that it was not very edible. An enraged individual signing himself 'A Christchurch Provision Dealer' wrote to *The Christchurch Times* with the observation that the transgressor 'will be offered better food in any prison in the country than he obtained at Fairmile House'. Other casuals tried to bring their own food in: this was also a punishable offence.

Punishments remained severe. A Swiss man, resident in this country for 27 years, was recommended for deportation by magistrates after a fight with an attendant, in addition to a sentence of 28 days for assault and 14 days for 'refractory conduct'.

At the Cottage Homes, the overcrowding was relieved by the opening of two new Homes (5 and 6) delayed by the war, in 1926. At the start of the war, about 150 children had been crammed into accommodation designed for half that number, so these were badly needed. Each new home cost £4,000; 'Everyone was delighted with the spick and span appearance,' enthused *The Christchurch Times*. One Home, Number 6, was to be pressed

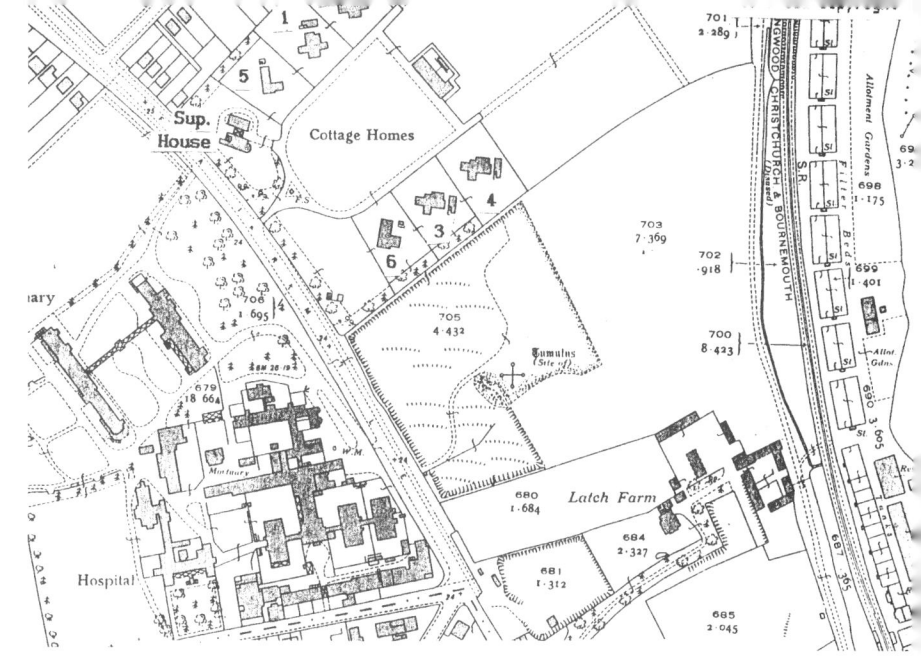

The site showing the infirmaries and new Cottage Homes. O.S.1946

into service as a nursery for the under-fives under the auspices of a 'specially trained official', Miss Perks. No expense was spared, apparently, to provide the new young residents with all they needed by way of dolls and other toys and pictures.

Some children could be boarded out still, but only if orphaned or deserted. One lucky boy was adopted by his foster-parents. Foster-parents were paid 10s per week, which caused some resentment among local families who had to raise their own children on far less. Others went as before to Canada, or Australia.

Life for the children went on as usual, with the occasional treat, for instance one arranged by the Bournemouth Rotary Club to the Theatre Royal. May Day was another occasion: once the children actually got across the road to Fairmile House as the Guardians wished to see them in their

CHRISTCHURCH UNION.

Superintendent of the Cottage Homes
September, 1922.

Admissions since 30th Sept., 1921 ... Total	61
Discharged to present date	62
Discharged as follows :—	
To relations	24
Boarded out	12
By removal orders to other Unions ...	3
Boys and Girls—Domestic service in hotels, &c.	5
Infirmary—all made a good recovery ...	6
To Sanitary Hospital—scarlet fever, ditto	4
Special Homes for mentally deficient children	3
„ Industrial Schools ...	1
„ T.S. Mercury for Royal Navy	1
„ By adoption	1
Emigrated to Canada (boys)	2
No deaths ...	-
Total	62

    1872 children have been dealt with at the Homes since 15th May, 1901 during the service of the present Supt. and Matron, Mr. and Mrs. Blakeborough, and during the whole period of 21 years and 4 months not a single child has died at the Homes.

    During the same period 1766 children have been discharged to relations and service, and quite 96 per cent. have done well and are now leading the lives of respectable citizenship, and less than a dozen have died including five who died fighting for their country during the Great War. Sixty old boys joined His Majesty's services during the War and there was not a single conscript amongst them.

    One old boy, now at Brixham, has got a full Captain's seamanship certificate and controlled a mines trawler in the Mediterranean during the war, and two boys are Warrant Officers in the Navy.

    The Scouts—3 patrols of 8 (total 24) have been well maintained during the past year.

    Girl Guides and Brownies (24) have been established during the past 12 months under Miss Froud and Miss Horrell, and these organisations have had a splendid effect on the present good tone and discipline at the Homes.

    Corporal punishment during the past year has been almost nil and so the good conduct all round has been a credit to our children and the staff. And the health of the children has been very good and illnesses rare for the past 21 years.

R. BLAKEBOROUGH.

11th September, 1922.

Report for the year ending September 1922

·CHRISTCHURCH·UNION·COTTAGE·HOMES·FAIRMILE·
·FOR·THE·BOARD·OF·GUARDIANS·
·BOYS·HOME·

fancy dress. The Cottage Homes Girl Guide troupe was invited to Highcliffe Castle to meet Queen Mary in 1928. Christmas continued to be very special for them, and one occasion when they would eat with real enthusiasm. In 1926, the 84 children apparently got through 600 oranges, cwt of pork, 20 dozen mince pies and 300 other cakes in two days! The Homes were decorated with great imagination: one had a winter scene recreated in the hall with Red Riding Hood and the wolf in bed and the dayroom decorated as Fairyland. Another Home that year (1929) featured a Woodland Wedding tableau, with intricate detail, such as a miniature

The Cottage Homes children at the National (Priory) School. Note the old-fashioned tunics, laced boots and plain haircuts.

illuminated church. The boys' Home featured a realistic fantasy garden complete with water-lilies and flower-beds. In the old schoolroom, a huge Christmas tree, donated as always by Lord Malmesbury, was covered in gifts.

In 1929, Clarendon Road School was opened, an event which led the Guardians into a furious confrontation with the Education Authority, which refused admission to Cottage Homes children (on grounds of space). Little children as young as five or six were having to walk down into the town to attend the Priory School - four times a day, as they came back for lunch, so it seemed only sensible and fair to allow them to attend the new and closer school. Indeed, in the words once again of *The Christchurch Times*, the Authority appeared to have 'barred, bolted and fortified' the school doors against them. The Guardians were defiant, even at one stage in the argument prepared to take direct action by taking the infants to Clarendon and challenging the school to expel them. Eventually, in the face of the Guardians' valiant campaign in the final weeks of their existence, the Education Authority gave way and allowed ten places for the infants.

The Blakeboroughs retired from the Cottage Homes in 1932 amidst tributes from the members of the defunct Board of Guardians. 95% of the children turned out well, said Mr Kitcher, and many of the ex-Cottage Homers returned to visit to show off new spouses and babies.

In the place of the Blakeboroughs came Mr Harry Dunn as Superintendant and his wife, Elizabeth, as Matron. Mr Dunn organised sports days every year on the Cottage Homes green. They were to be the last holders of these posts.

Memories of a Cottage Home inmate.

Not many people who grew up in the Cottage Homes are willing to talk about those days. Their memories are of being jeered at at in the school playground, of wearing identical clothing, of not having parents and not knowing normal family life. Fortunately, one lady was prepared to speak out and the following is based on her account.

This lady arrived at the Homes in the early twenties, her parents being alive but not able to support her or her brothers and sisters. Her father was in Fairmile House, and she was able to visit him there once a week, but had no contact with her mother. Conscious though she was of her poverty, she was nevertheless aware that she was better off in the Home than the children of the slums in Pound Lane or the Pit site.

This lady remembers the interiors of the Homes - the polished vitreous flooring, the forms in the dining hall, the plain but nutritious food. She left at the outbreak of the second world war, but still remembers the unvarying meal routine of soup and fruit pudding on Monday, fish on Tuesday, roast meat on Wednesday, soup and an orange on Thursday, suet pudding on Friday and a roast again on Sunday. She must be forgiven for not remembering Saturday's fare!

Every child had a number, and this was on their pegs and sewn into all their clothes. She remembers wearing ribbed stockings, button boots, serge dresses and pinnies, but also remembers that Mrs Dunn very quickly made improvements to the girls' clothing after she arrived in 1932, arranging for them to wear prettier dresses, which they greatly appreciated. Ten children slept in each dormitory, which had a spyhole in the door. Outside were extensive grounds, cultivated by labour from Fairmile House, and the piggeries. The children used the old schoolhouse as a hall; it had a stage that they used for plays and other activities such as Girl Guides. The shoemaker had a workshop in another part of the school. The lady who was the Guide leader was one of the kinder adults to come into contact with the Cottage Home children - Miss Froud, of the boot and shoe family well known in the town in these and earlier days.

The children largely made their own fun. The excursions, such as they were, consisted of an annual trip on the tram to Bournemouth to see the 'pictures'- incredibly, it was always the same film - Scrooge! Her memories of other officials are not so warm: the Blakeboroughs were hard in their dealings with the children, as perhaps was to be expected of those whose values were formed in the Victorian age. The Dunns were kinder; Mrs Dunn in particular being a warm-hearted person. Mr Peaty, the fiery socialist, is remembered with amusement as the Guardian who instructed the young children not to stand for the National Anthem: as this went against the orders of the other Guardians, much confusion arose! Discipline was strict, and the children were treated rather impersonally - there were simply too many of them, she recalls, for individual attention to be given. Years later, when in service in Christchurch, she glimpsed her employers cradling their new baby in their arms by the fireside, and realised what she had missed out on in a normal family life, with the warmth and affection all children have the right to expect.

Discipline sometimes involved cruelty - physical punishment. One poor girl who accidentally wet her bed was beaten with a batten of wood. On this occasion, my informant had the courage to bring this incident to the attention of the Guardians when they visited and ritually enquired whether there were any complaints; the assistant concerned was dismissed as a result. It was this strength of spirit that enabled some children like this lady to come through this institutional upbringing relatively unscathed. Others were far more affected emotionally, and it would be wrong to omit that there is a suggestion that some girls experienced being molested whilst at the Homes.

During the same period, a small boy came into the Cottage Homes and has similar memories. He especially remembers the concrete yard between the Home and the wash-house which had to be scrubbed down each and every day by the boys. His Home, Number Two, had a typical layout of kitchen and dining rooms downstairs, with a store for the boots and shoes, and the dormitory upstairs. The wash-house outside also featured a coal house and the latrines.

The grounds were tended by workhouse labour, and included a kitchen garden on the site of the present Queensmead. At the rear of the Cottage Homes land was the piggery; every week one was killed on the site and carted over, draped with a bloodied cover, to the workhouse kitchen opposite.

The schoolroom housed the dentist, the gardener (Mr Seymour) and the shoemaker (Mr Hopkins), and was used as a schoolroom during the second world war, presumably as an overspill for Clarendon Road school.

He had a brother and a sister in the Homes, but as they were brought up separately he grew apart from them. School was at Clarendon Road, where the Cottage Homes children were invariably blamed for any misdeeds. The uniform consisted of blue or grey trousers and jersey, and a red and black tie.

One day, this small boy played truant from school. Not knowing where to go to escape detection in his distinctive uniform, he sat down in despair at the side of the road in Fairmile, next to a milestone. As his hands touched the ground, he was surprised and delighted to feel them touch a coin: the grand sum of tuppence. This little boy rushed down to the '2/6d store' (Woolworths) in the town to purchase a rare treat of a sweet. With his prize in his hand, he sought cover by a haystack at Latch Farm. Alas, when he opened his treat, he discovered to his dismay that all he had purchased was a packet of cream crackers. He ate them, dry as they were, all the same.

His most abiding memory, and most profound regret for his childhood, was never having had a goodnight kiss.

Memories of a Cottage Home 'Foster Mother'

Miss W. Coffin was put in charge of Home No. 2 at the young age of 22 in 1936, although she has memories of the Homes going back to the mid-twenties. At that time, she recalls that her grandmother, who was employed there, took 'direct action' against Mr Blakeborough by snapping the cane that he was about to use on an offending boy. Food during those days was strictly no frills: thick bread doorstops with mugs of cocoa were the staple diet. The arrival of Mr and Mrs Dunn brought a softer regime. One of the first changes was the exchange of boots for shoes.

Foster-mother was the new name for 'matron', and they were known to the children as 'Aunty'. The foster-mothers had a great deal of autonomy, and so the atmosphere of each home very much depended on the Aunty's character and methods. For instance, Miss Coffin went to some trouble to prepare something tasty from the meat allowance; in other Homes it would simply be placed in the oven to cook as it was.

The boys still had a uniform of sorts, consisting of a grey shirt with navy and red tie and a cap to match with red cord, worn with trousers of varying colour. In the summer they wore khaki-coloured shorts with shirts again of various colours. The girls did not appear to have identical clothes.

Many of the children came from seriously deprived backgrounds and some were very sad cases. They were better off in the Cottage Homes than with their families, and also better off than being boarded out, as this was often only done for financial gain. More than forty years after the Cottage Homes were closed, Miss Coffin still receives correspondence and visits from the men who grew up in her Home; proof that some of the children from this period had reason to feel real affection for the place of their upbringing and for the staff who had done their best to give them a secure and happy childhood.

CHAPTER THIRTEEN

the NHS

It was apparent that another war was on its way. VAD nurses were once again at Fairmile, practising air-raid drills on the green in the centre of the Cottage Homes. Once again, Miss Hamilton was a Commandant and a Miss Beech-Johnston her assistant, together with a Lady-Superintendant, Miss Heriot-Hill. They also erected a hospital ward in the schoolhouse, all of which activity received hearty commendation from the visiting War Office inspector, Major Newland.

Once war broke out, Fairmile House was once again pressed into service to help wounded soldiers. This time the injuries referred to did not seem on quite the dramatic scale as in the first world war: instead of 'trench foot', inmates had a variety of minor disorders, some very odd indeed, such as the patient with a 'hysterical shoulder'. There is an account of these times from one of the soldiers treated there, from which we learn that two wards were used for the Emergency Hospital, mainly for army patients, who relished being away from the military discipline usually a feature of army hospitals. So much so, it would appear, that high spirits would erupt into pillow fights and the like, which the appearance of one Sister Burnett usually quelled. The soldier-patient remembers the lovely grounds, immaculately kept and complete with a bowling green. The Cottage Homes played a role too in the war, receiving children evacuated from Southampton.

Life for the inmates went on as before, it would seem, though concerts and suchlike had become rather scarce. Christmas was still a big occasion, both here and at the Cottage Homes, and the mayors of both Christchurch and Bournemouth would attend to help serve the food to the inmates, who numbered about 450 (excluding the Cottage Homes) in 1944.

Soldiers (and friends) relaxing

It seems that the old people of Christchurch were still having to go to Fordingbridge, as one lady wrote to *The Christchurch Times* about the difficulties this was creating for relatives wishing to visit them. Christchurch Council was also pressing for this to be changed - it was a consequence of Fairmile House being run by Bournemouth Council since the abolition of the Guardians in 1930. The day seemed to have been won by 1949.

It was after the war that Fairmile House faced the next major upheaval, and it was one that was resisted by local people just as fiercely as the Guardians resisted the 1930 upheaval. This was, of course, the creation of the welfare state in 1948, and the transformation of the institution to a hospital.

On 15th July of that year, the entire Poor Law was abolished. Out went the Public Assistance Board, in came the National Assistance Board. Poor Law relief became National Assistance, which was a state and not a local provision. Swept away with it was the whole paraphernalia of settlement rules and contributions from relatives for those being maintained in Poor Law institutions and the removal of pensions for the same purpose from inmates receiving them. Not that the Guardians of the old days had entirely disappeared from the scene: Mr Peaty and another Bournemouth ex-Guardian, Mrs Saye, served on the Welfare Committee of Bournemouth Council and thus continued to play a part in the developing hospital.

A Regional Hospital Board was created, but administered for a while by the Fairmile Agency Committee, the job of which was to wind up the previous Public Assistance Committee and lead into the Hospital Management Committee. Bureaucracy still flourished.

The first act of the new Board was to attempt to transfer all the aged people, so inconveniently using beds that now had 'hospital' labels on them, out to St Leonard's Hospital, originally a wartime hospital for the American air force, near Ringwood. This move did not endear the new authority to the people of Christchurch and Bournemouth. Even the old Poor Law officers railed against the plan: 'It would seem', wrote Mr Morgan, so recently the Master of Fairmile House, 'the planners under the despised

Haig Ward at Christmas

Poor Law had bigger hearts and more enterprise than those with the "new look".' A Bournemouth councillor, Mr Owen Ellum, joined in vociferously, praising Fairmile House as 'a splendid building, well-managed and . . . the envy of all local authorities. The inmates look happy,, well fed and well housed . . . Some of the people have been there a very long time . . . and they regard it as a happy home.' He called a public meeting, where Mr Peaty accused the Board of the 'utmost cruelty' in their desire to move the old people out, and paid tribute to Mr Morgan who, he said, would have prevented the loss of Fairmile House to the hospital service had he still been the Master. 'The powers-that-be', he claimed, 'would never have been able to manipulate things as they did and try to make out that the

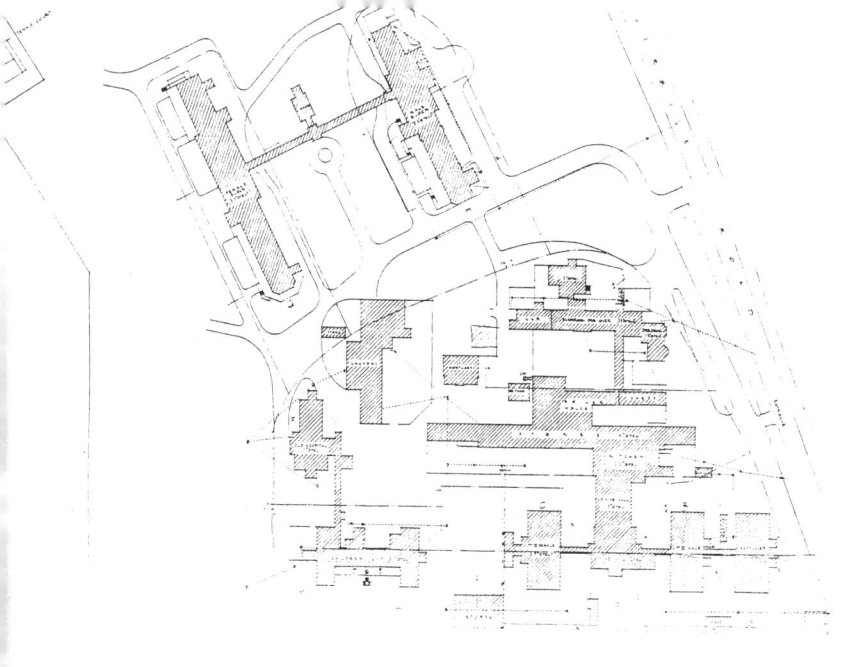

The new hospital, 1952 soon after the NHS takeover
By the Bournemouth and East Dorset Hospital Management Company

major use of Fairmile House was for sick people.' Joining in the fray, a Mr Cogswell stirringly reminded his audience that: 'Are not some of these people the sturdy old folk of England, who raised their families without any assistance from the State? Their children were raised without any free milk or schools and without family allowances. Perhaps if they had had some of these things, they would not be where they are now.'

Christchurch Council joined in the protests, as did the patients, who organised a petition to the King and Queen and the Prime Minister, Mr Churchill. A member of the Regional Hospital Board accused the organisers of forging the signatures! The local Labour Party also took up the issue and wrote in support to the Ministry of Health.

The beds were needed so that the Hospital Board could add surgical facilities. The battle against this 'medicalising' of Fairmile House was fought hard. Mr Morgan referred to previous attempts to grab the best wards, 'to oust those for whom they were designed and built, and the attempts were made just because the old Board of Guardians had made such a good job of them.' Surgical cases had always gone to Boscombe - the Royal Victoria Hospital (demolished about 1992). It had been a voluntary hospital. This arrangement left Fairmile House with the chronically sick and infirm, and it was this position that the objectors sought to maintain. Mr Peaty was again in the forefront of opposition, supporting Mr Morgan's view that 'the medical facility have had their eye on [Fairmile House] for many years'.

Aneurin Bevan himself replied for the Ministry of Health. He declined to meet a planned deputation and backed the Hospital Board. All looked quite hopeless, but out of the blue in 1949 the Fairmile Protest Committee, as they had styled themselves, was advised by the Ministry that the scheme was being abandoned indefinitely because of - the Ministry claimed - capital expenditure cutbacks. It was never revived, but the Board found another place in which to decant the elderly . . .

After the opposition was subdued, Fairmile Hospital, as it was now titled, became the focus of an intensive programme of refurbishment and expansion. The training school for nurses, in the old original lying-in ward attached to the first workhouse infirmary, expanded and built up an excellent reputation. It was in 1949 the first school of its kind in the county, and grew from a role of nine trainee nurses in 1951 to 92 pupils and three teachers in 1967.

The accommodation for the nurses was constantly being improved and modernised, the 'old Poor Law furniture' being dispensed with in 1956 and a new Nurses' Home opened in 1964. This was named Trinidad House in recognition of all the Commonwealth nurses who were trained at Christchurch Hospital, and opened by Sir Learie Constantine, the West Indies cricketer. By 1954, six years after the creation of the National Health Service, an article in *The Christchurch Times* described the hospital as having 'modern and comprehensive equipment' but no operating facility or out-patients department, apart from physiotherapy. A children's

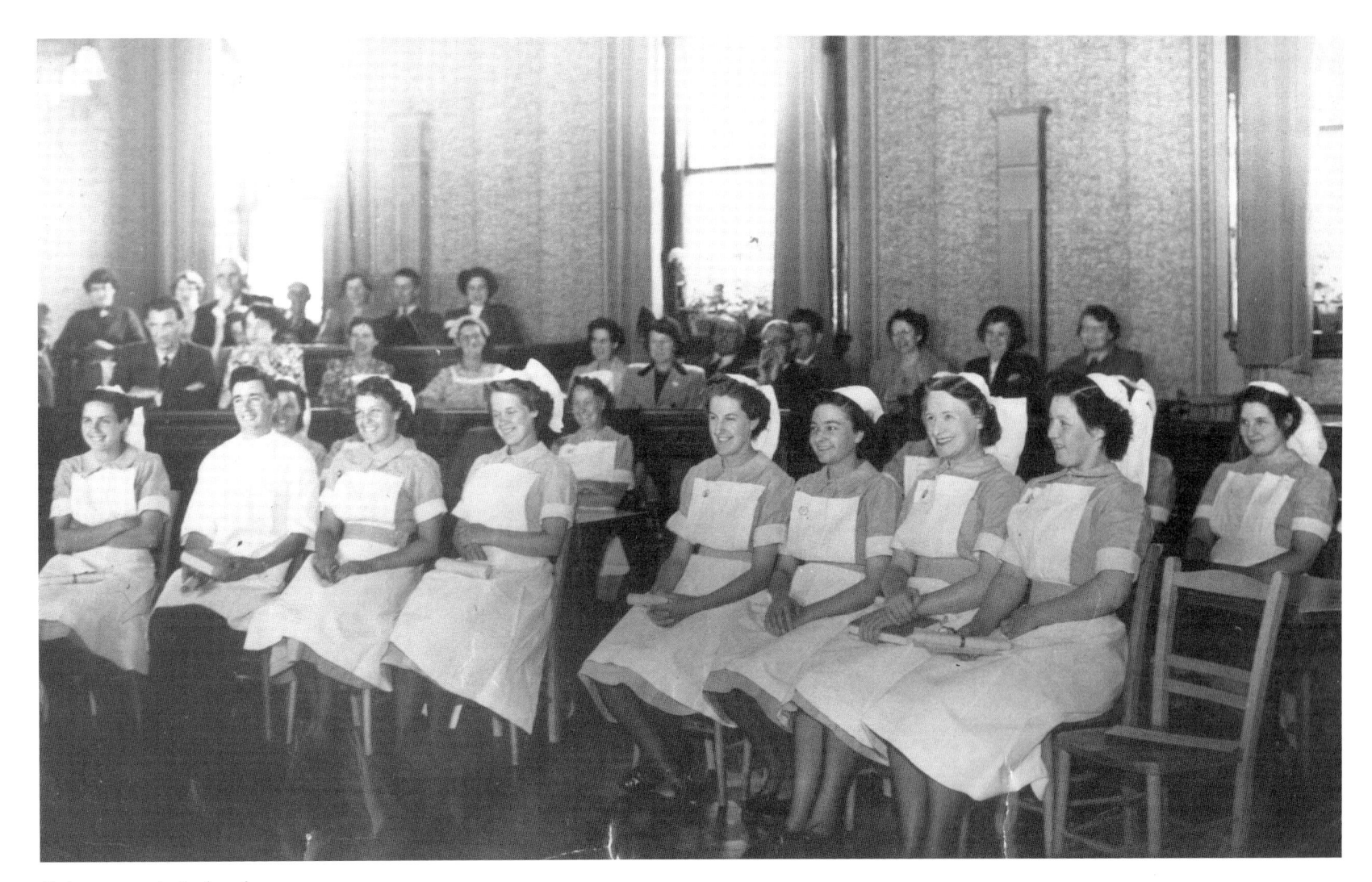

Trainee nurses in the boardroom.

Christmas 1956, staff include Matron Miss Lewy (extreme left); Mr Horace Scott, chairman of House Committee, behind, Cllr Ken Smith left of centre. Behind him is hospital secretary Mr Geoffrey Guy. Centre front: Sister Bennett.

ward had developed, and by a quirk of fate had been put in the very same building where the Red House children had come to in 1886. At the time of the NHS takeover, there was some sort of a nursery, as Bournemouth Council's Children's Committee minutes refer to a provision for the under-3s, especially those 'deprived of a normal life'. When Poole General Hospital opened in 1969, the children's unit was closed down and the children transferred there, wherupon the old school accommodation/children's ward was converted into the Day Hospital for the elderly.

The Grand Plan for equipping Christchurch Hospital as a General Hospital was unveiled in 1955, and involved a scheme to the tune of £77,000 to provide a surgical operating theatre in G Block. This was duly opened in 1957 by the Mayor of Christchurch, Cllr Ken Smith, who was also the nephew of Guardian Mrs Shave, and by the Bournemouth Mayor, Cllr Templeman. Echoes of the past were also invoked with the arrival of Red

The 'Floral Corridor' this was alongside the dining hall and dated from the Workhouse era. (Courtesy The Nursing Mirror, 1953).

Female Medical Ward – G block 1953 (Courtesy The Nursing Mirror).

Cross ladies on the wards, though now they were distributing confectionery and magazines instead of bandages and Woodbines.

By 1961, the old inmates' dining hall had been converted for staff (most regrettably with the installation of a false ceiling which today partially obscures the lovely stained glass motifs) and the kitchens upgraded, H Block modernised to include central heating, new bathrooms and floors and the laundry once again extended and modernised. Incredibly, one inmate remained throughout these transformations: Miss Nellie Farnham, aged 77, who had been admitted way back in 1924, in the days of the Board of Guardians. 35 years later, Miss Farnham, who had rheumatoid arthritis, said, 'The hospital has changed very little. There have been redecorations, new beds and furniture, but apart from the new surgical unit, the main buildings have remained much the same.' She felt that hospital life today was rather more 'official' than in the old days, but 'there is still the personal touch about the place'.

The redecoration to which Miss Farnham referred was described in *The Christchurch Times* as 'quite unlike the severe black, white and olive green "barracks" of a decade ago [i.e. during the war] but now glowing with subdued pastels, bedspreads of pink, peach and green, nurses' outfits in light mauve with white aprons, and green tunics for male nurses; Sisters have dark blue with white aprons, Matron has maroon.' The children's unit, it went on to say, had French grey on one wall, peach and beige on another; others are turquoise and honeysuckle . . . ' So much for the taste of the fifties!

The hospital grounds soon found more buildings springing up in place of the ornamental grounds, notably the John Farmer school for the mentally handicapped, alongside the old children's block in Jumpers Road (1959).

Once the old people had been moved on - the story of this follows at the end of the chapter - there remained only one more problem in the way of the new hospital's up-to-date image, and that was the tramps. They were annoying many people by then - by clambering through the hedge by the Nurses' Home, which they appeared to regard as a short cut, by disturbing local residents and even those across the road in the Cottage Homes, with their drunken behaviour at night (they were meant to be inside between 9pm and 5am, but the hospital authority was ineffective in this respect), by damaging property and offending with bad language. Female tramps would turn up and be turned away, since it had become the policy at some stage only to admit men.

Each day, a maximum of about 70 and a minimum of about 30 of them would turn up at the 'Reception Centre' - its post-NHS designation. Mr Morgan encapsulated the new situation in a speech to a local Conservative Association in 1951: 'Lots of things have been said about the Poor Law, but one thing it did was to ensure that anyone in need did receive assistance, and it did ensure that idleness was not encouraged. If wayfarers took advantage of the accommodation, they were required to do a job of work unless they could show that they had work to go to. Under this new Act . . . the position is that vagrants can frequent institutions and need not be required to do a job of work. Everything is made easy for them.'

Certainly, what work was required of them was a whole lot easier - maybe some cleaning, some gardening, washing dishes or vegetables, or at worst, some wood-chopping. Not that the usual refusals were not heard and duly met with short prison sentences. Mr Ken Smith, then a magistrate, said that on the first offence all that was done was to reprimand the recalcitrant tramp. So different from the summary justice of seven days hard labour as of yore.

In 1956, the Christchurch Hospital Management Committee said in their report: 'We have had enough of the Reception Centre, but realise the people who occupy it have a rightful place in the world.' It was decided that this rightful place was at Hurn, to a 'spike' as such places were mysteriously nicknamed, somewhere in Matchams Lane, which Hurn Parish Council valiantly offered for this use for an initial three-year period.

So, by 1967, there was but one vestige of workhouse days only - one small stretch of chocolate-brown corridor.

After all this fever of activity, it seems incredible that the Ministry of Health should have sought to downgrade the hospital - now a general

Another group of Cottage Homes children – still in outdated smocks.

hospital - to a geriatric unit. Massive public opposition was once again mustered; 10,000 signatures were collected on a petition organised by the Christchurch Hospital League of Friends (established in 1954) and once again a deputation was refused, this time by Minister Kenneth Robinson. He dismissed the campaign as 'emotional'. Writing in *The Christchurch Times*, journalist Jack Dwyer pointed out that 'our hospital is the well-balanced, happy organism it is BECAUSE it has so many departments.' Once again, the campaigners proved victorious.

Last of the Cottage Homes

As soon as the NHS took over Christchurch Hospital in 1948, Bournemouth Council directed their attention to the Cottage Homes. This was not a predatory move, but a response to the changing way in which the care of children was being regarded. It was no longer considered to be in the best interests of such children to be raised in an institution.

All seemed to carry on as before, except that there was no longer a Superintendant. Mr Dunn had died at the young age of 49, nine years into the job. He had done much for the children, having instituted the annual sports day, become scoutmaster of the Fairmile Troop, as it was known, and on the whole acted as a father to the Cottage Homes children, as Mrs Grimes observed to her fellow Public Assistance Committee members on his death in 1941. His obituary in *The Christchurch Times* praised 'his kindly discipline and flair for organisation, which had raised the tone of the Homes to a high standard, the children being well-mannered and orderly.' He had also taken a prominent role in the town, so typical of those Fairmile House officials, being a member of the town's football club and amateur dramatic society and also a singer. Mrs Dunn was to continue alone; she was the same kind of person with public commitments over and above her position in the Homes - for many years being chairman of the Christchurch Townswomens' Guild, a Civil Defence Officer during the war, a freemason and a Red Cross worker. Sadly, they lost a son during the war.

Mrs Dunn, according to a source who was brought up in the Homes in the forties, was an exceptionally caring person, but may have been somewhat naive about some of the other members of staff, particularly the 'aunties' who were in charge of the individual Homes. The abuse that was coming to light earlier continued unabated. Furthermore, pilfering of supplies was apparently common, which included literally taking the sweets from the mouths of babes - their sweet rations were allegedly appropriated. Punishments were devised to humiliate children: bedwetters were forced to stand in a corner with the damp sheet over their head. Whilst the children spent their after-school hours mending their socks before going to bed early, some of the staff amused themselves drinking in their rooms, and any bad tempers were inevitably taken out on their young charges.

The outside world regarded the Cottage Homes children with mixed feelings, recalls my informant. They seemed to suffer from an undeserved poor reputation, being often the first suspects at school whenever a misdemeanour was discovered; on the other hand, many kinder people would take the children out on excursions, and at Christmas and Easter they would receive gifts galore.

Education was provided by Stourfield School in Southbourne, to which the children walked daily. This school was very good to the children on the whole, but no encouragement in their studies was given back at the Homes, as a result of which homework was rarely done. Sundays were church days: a walk to the Priory, sometimes twice, and another walk to St George's in Jumpers Road.

Life still had its pleasures, nevertheless. In the summer there were regular picnic excursions to the river nearby, and throughout the year the dining hall at Fairmile House was used for film shows. A weekly visit to a youth club at Pokesdown was permitted, and the big annual events such as bonfire night and sports day were eagerly looked forward to.

This brief account of life at the Homes in those days is a reminder that childrens's homes scandals are not a modern phenomenon. It suggest that insufficient attention was paid by the authorities to the proper training and supervision of the Cottage Homes staff, as a result of which the kind of person attracted to these posts were sometimes ill-educated and temperamentally unsuited to work that required patience and integrity.

All seemed as usual at the start of the fifties, except that the Homes had been renamed as The Bournemouth Children's Homes. The outings continued much as before - a visit to Weymouth, summer camp at New Romney, Kent, a children's party hosted by the newly-formed Christchurch lodge of the Royal Order of Moose, and so on.

But change was in the air. No 3 Home's closure was discussed by the Children's Committee as early as 1949. The reason was the new enlightenment: children were to go to foster homes when at all possible. The same fate was being planned for Homes 1 and 2 not much later. Whilst these deliberations were in hand, the committee approached the main Bournemouth Council with the offer to hand over the Homes for use by elderly and infirm people currently clogging up wards earmarked at the hospital for surgical cases. That sealed their fate, and gave the hospital management authorities the solution to the problem with old people that had caused so much controversy only shortly beforehand. The end, when it came, was sudden. Mrs Dunn was offered alternative work, but none suited, and she retired, the tribute from the Children's Committee ('ability and loyalty . . . kindness and affection to many children . . . ') ringing in her ears. She died in 1956. The Homes were to close to the children 31st March 1952. The same month the Homes were rechristened Queens Close, furniture was removed from the Elizabeth Wood Home of Rest at the hospital, lino was laid, radiators installed, and about 100 old people made the move across the road to their new hostel in July. What they felt about it history has failed to record. It was the obligation of Regional Hospital Boards to provide hostel-type accommodation for such elderly people, and hostels were in fact springing up all over the area. The responsibility towards children was also defined under the 1948 Children's Act which dictated that all local authority children should be boarded out.

The coup was reported in *The Bournemouth Times:* 'Bournemouth Corporation Children's Committee has been so successful in boarding out boys and girls under their care into decent, private homes that they have been able to close down their Christchurch Cottage Homes . . . More than 100 young people in these Homes have been found foster-parents.' The Children's Officer for the borough commented that it showed how much Bournemouth people have supported them in their search for good homes. The children were to be visited regularly and strictly supervised, just as they had been all along since the practice was first adopted in Mr Blandford's day. Not all of the children found such homes: some were in council premises in 53 Wellington Road, Bournemouth, or 12 Suffolk Road, and some at a nursery at Southbourne.

There was, of course, no use for the land and piggeries, which were therefore let out. There was also no further use for the children's swings, which went to the Bournemouth Council Childrens and Parks Committee.

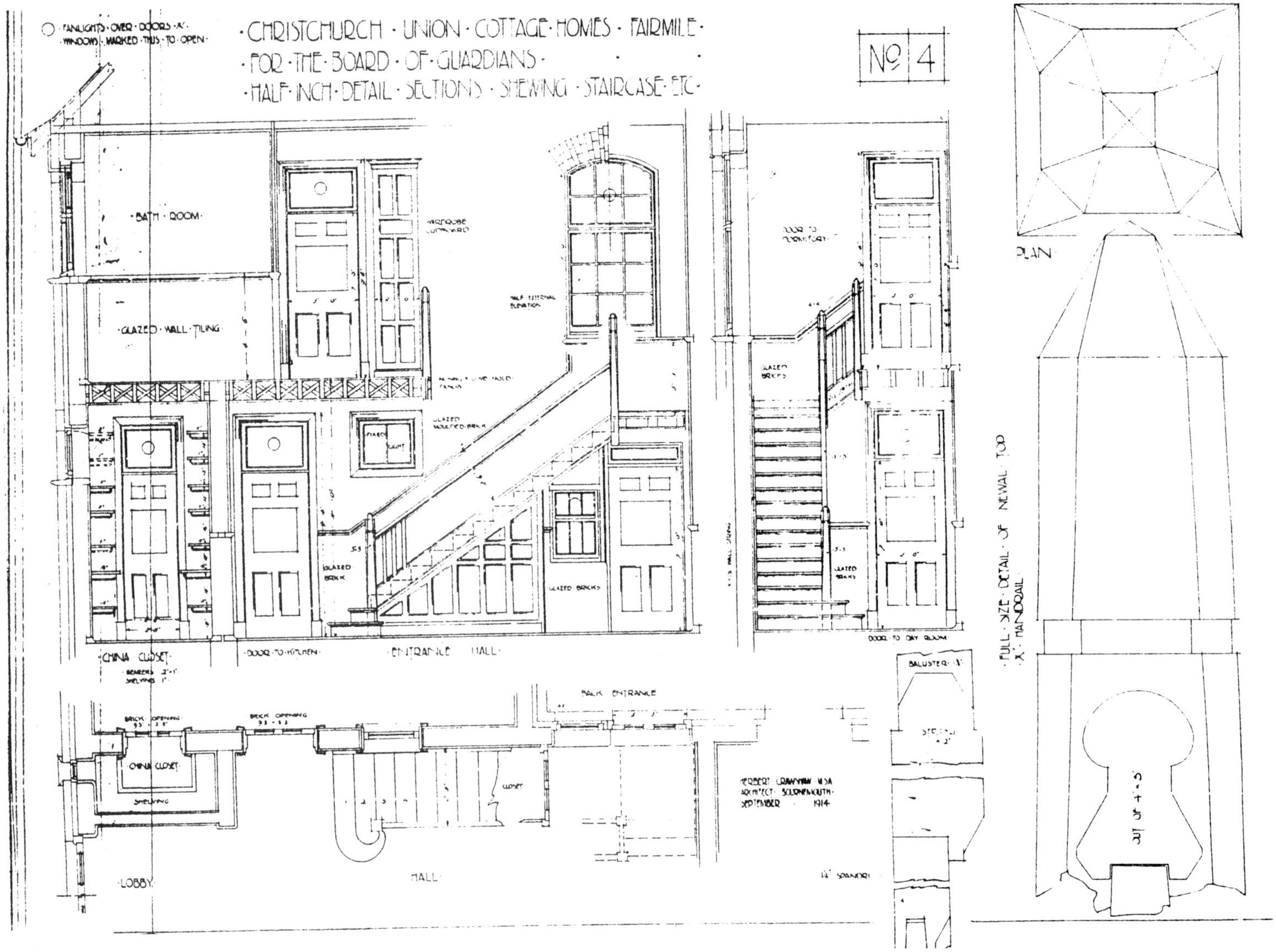
·CHRISTCHURCH · UNION · COTTAGE · HOMES · FAIRMILE ·
·FOR · THE · BOARD · OF · GUARDIANS ·
·HALF · INCH · DETAIL · SECTIONS · SHEWING · STAIRCASE · ETC ·
No 4
·BATH · ROOM ·
·GLAZED · WALL · TILING ·
CHINA · CLOSET
DOOR · TO · KITCHEN
ENTRANCE · HALL
BACK · ENTRANCE
CHINA · CLOSET
SHELVING
LOBBY
HALL
DOOR · TO · DAY · ROOM
BALUSTER
PLAN
·FULL · SIZE · DETAIL · OF · NEWAL · TOP
·X· HANDRAIL
HERBERT · CRAWSHAW · M.S.A
ARCHITECT · BOURNEMOUTH
SEPTEMBER · 1914

Around 1957, the old schoolroom from the Cottage Homes days seems to have enjoyed a new and rather unsavoury role as the dumping ground for Bournemouth's problem families, who appear to have lived alongside whatever old people remained in the Queen's Close hostels at this time. This came to the attention of *The Christchurch Herald*. In a 'shock horror' front-page splash the paper tried to wake up Christchurch people to the situation prevailing in what was, after all, part of Christchurch even though it had by then been under Bournemouth for years. 'Appalling Conditions' screamed the headline, going on to make allegations about families living in sub-standard conditions, cramped, without hot water or storage facilities, with prowling tramps at all hours from the Reception Centre. They appeared to have been people evicted from Bournemouth council houses. Cllr Tucker complained to the Ministry of Health and returned hopeful. His optimism was justified: a damaged sink got repaired and an additional refuse bin was provided.

The first Home to be bulldozed according to Bournemouth Council minutes was No 4, which made way in 1965 for Avon View. This latest home, reported *The Christchurch Times*, was 'raised, ironically, on the site of a provision of the old Poor Law, which many people dreaded - the workhouse . . . The Director of Welfare Services says the cottage-type homes at Christchurch - retained only for emergency - will disappear when the second home is built . . .'

Next to go was No 7 - not a number that was used, but possibly the schoolroom. As promised, Queensmead Old People's Home was up in 1967. Three more Homes went in 1965; the Superintendant's Home (recently let to hospital doctors) in 1966; and the last Home, No 2, in 1966. Homes 5 and 6 were less than forty years old, and contained fittings of high quality when constructed - it seems such a waste. This sequence may have been put into operation in a different order, but accurate information on this point, or, indeed, photographs of the Homes, does not exist.

The buildings thus cursorily disposed of, the question remained of what to do with all the land - about 17 acres of it. Something of a wrestling match then ensued between two Bournemouth Council committees: the Housing Committee and the Welfare Services Committee. Plans for development had been discussed with the County Council (which at that time had to be approached if a planning application involved more than 5 acres), but Christchurch Council was not enthusiastic. The Welfare Committee claimed the cost of the land if the Housing Committee acquired it; it became an uneconomic proposition then. In 1969, Bournemouth Council submitted an application to Christchurch for 210 homes, which was approved. 'The biggest single housing scheme in Christchurch's history', in the words of Bournemouth planners, went ahead, and Queens Close passed into history in favour of Bronte Avenue, Emily Close, and so forth.

I am told by an apparently normal young lady whose home is in Emily Close, site of Home No 5, that the sound of children can be heard in the empty upstairs bedrooms.

The lady who grew up in these Homes told me that the children had a game in their dormitory, climbing in and out of bed . . .

conclusion

It is easy for us now to look back on the days of the workhouse with a mixture of morbid fascination and amused contempt. It seems barbaric that conditions in the workhouses should have been made so unpleasant, as if the poor and disadvantaged, as we now call them, did not have enough brutality in their daily lives.

It would, though, be judging our forebears too harshly if we did not take into account the inadequacy, even absence, of health care which the workhouse infirmaries gradually came to redress. Nor must we ignore the service that was provided for the aged, in the days before universal pensions, when Christchurch Workhouse became for so many the only shelter that was to be had, and was much appreciated for that.

And looking around ourselves today, can we really feel so proud of our provision now? In every city in Britain, destitute people sleep out in the open in cardboard boxes. Some of them - a significant proportion, maybe even the majority - are discarded fron mental institutions with insufficient or absent aftercare. Is this in any way progress from the enforced incarceration in the casual wards? Whilst our present-day tramps are not put on back-breaking stone-pounding duties, neither do they have food and washing facilities when it is needed.

We still have not been able to solve the perennial problem of the able-bodied shirkers; in fact, the present benefit system makes it easy to depend on the State and give nothing in return.

Christchurch was fortunate in having Guardians of the Poor who were, on the whole, doing their best for the people in their charge, in the light of contemporary attitudes and legislation. Nowhere have I found anything akin to the abuses exposed at other workhouses. For, example, at Andover, the Master expropriated the funds and starved the inmates so severely that they were reduced to gnawing at old bones. which they were supposed to pound to powder as their task work. There is no record of children having been flogged senseless, such as happened in the workhouse that Sir Henry Stanley absconded from. The worst episode in the history of our workhouse, the death of John Campbell, was largely the result of mistakes, and was both greatly regretted by the Guardians and the subject of a meticulous inquiry by the inspector.

The legacy of the Cottage Homes is more complicated. Whilst evidence has been obtained of serious malpractices, it must be remembered that similar children's homes scandals have occurred in contemporary Britain.

Christchurch Workhouse evolved into a fine hospital, highly regarded by local people, and a very important asset to the town. It is to be hoped that the interesting collection of buildings at the hospital site will one day get the recognition they deserve and stand alongside the Red House Museum as a monument to the 'care in the community' policies of times past.

POSTSCRIPT

later hospital history

The most recent phase of expansion of the hospital was launched in 1970: £660,000 was to be spent on turning it into a major rehabilitation and assessment centre for the Wessex Regional Hospital Board area. The single-storey building between G and H Blocks was the result; unfortunately, the glass corridor and a magnificent old chestnut tree were sacrificed in the process.

The plan below shows the new buildings that were added as a result: Forest Dene rehabilitation unit, wards J, K and M, the MacMillan cancer-care unit, that has proved to be such an asset to Christchurch, the twin orthopaedic operating unit, and a gymnasium and hydrotherapy pool, and further facilities in the block built on the site of the glass corridor between blocks G and H.

In 1992, the long-awaited Royal Bournemouth Hospital was opened in Castle Lane, Tuckton. Christchurch Hospital then lost its theatres. This building is in the process of being converted into a new day centre.

At the time of writing, May 1994, the NHS Trust are seeking permission to demolish almost all of the workhouse buildings constructed before 1900 and described in Chapter Seven.

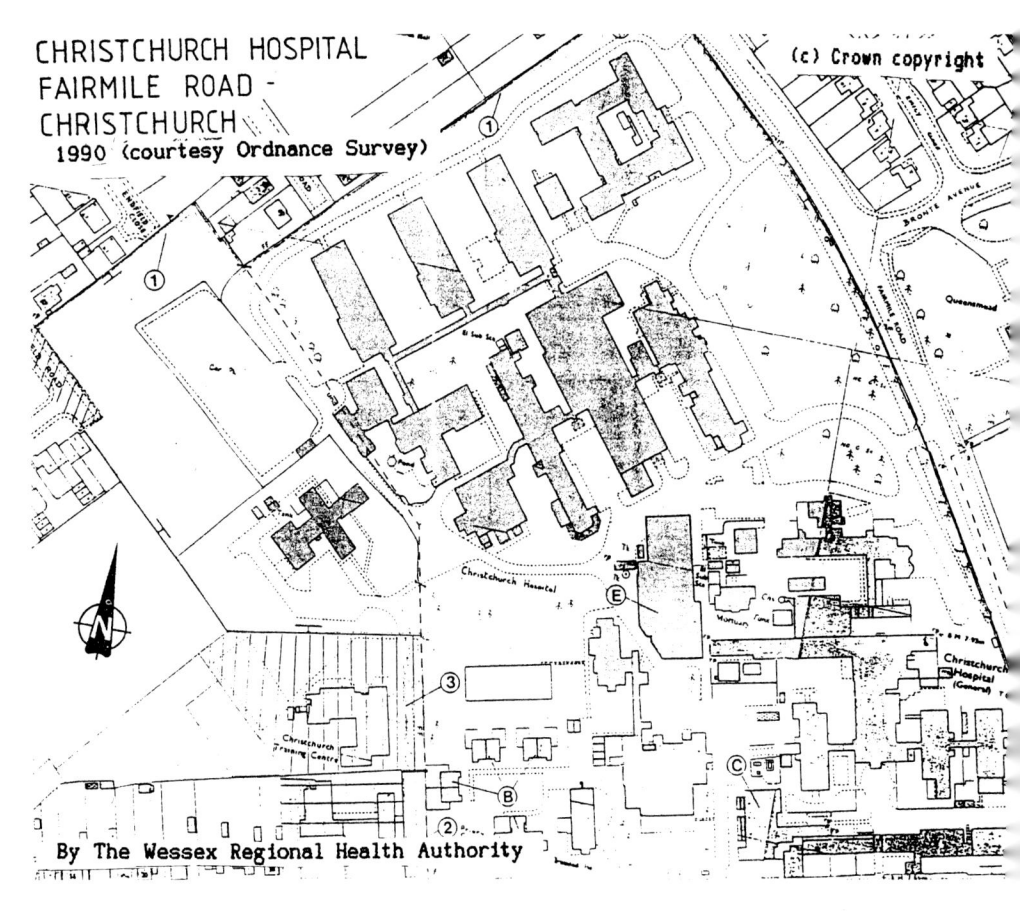

CHRISTCHURCH HOSPITAL
FAIRMILE ROAD - CHRISTCHURCH
1990 (courtesy Ordnance Survey)

By The Wessex Regional Health Authority

bibliography

Bingley Rev. *The History of Christchurch*, 1813

Druitt, Herbert *A Christchurch Miscellany*, 1924

Dyson, Taylor *A History of Christchurch*, 1954

Graham, Mary *The Royal National Hospital*, 1992

The Hampshire Archivists' Group *Poor Law in Hampshire through the Centuries*, 1970

Longham, Norman *The Workhouse*, 1974

Tucker, C. *A Historical and Descriptive Account of the Town and Borough of Christchurch*, 1837

Tucker, William *Reminiscences of Christchurch and Neighbourhood,* 1921

White, Allen *The Chain Makers*, 1967

Young, J.A. *Southbourne and Tuckton Yesterday*, 1990

Other sources include, of course, *The Christchurch Times, The Christchurch Herald, The Bournemouth Times, The Hampshire Magazine,* vestry records, workhouse records and plans held in the Dorset Record Office and at Christchurch Hospital, Bournemouth Council records and various papers housed in the Local History Room at Christchurch Library.

the 'underclass of today' ...

Prisoners' output replaces imports

By Ian Hamilton Fazey, Northern Correspondent

Prisoners are making their growing contribution to improving Britain's balance of payments by manufacturing goods previously imported into the country - and helping change attitudes to work among staff and inmates.

Longer working days and higher pay are being encouraged and prison enterprises are making a growing contribution to prison running costs.

Strangeways prison in Manchester - refurbished at a cost of £80m after being almost destroyed four years ago in Britain's worst prison riot - yesterday announced a 35-hour working week for prisoners.

The prison has negotiated a contract with a Warrington company to make 2,000 polypropylene bulk containers a week, undercutting a supplier in Turkey. Import substitution is one way to expand output without arousing allegations of cheap prison labour undercutting outside suppliers and destroying local jobs.

The containers - used for moving granular or powder products in palletised loads - are to be marketed throughout Europe.

Other Strangeways prisoners carry out upholstery for a local furniture company which used to buy finished products from France; now it imports the wooden frames, which are completed in the prison workshops.

The Strangeways laundry has so many orders that Mr Pat Smith, the manager, says he is starting double-shift working. Customers include restaurants in Manchester's Chinatown and Barnados children's homes. The prisoners earn as much as £10 a week.

There is another reward for co-operative behaviour at Strangeways - a television set in the cell, which must be paid for from prison earnings.

Extracts with kind permission of *The Financial Times* (28.5.94)

Report beggars to the police, PM tells public

By Ivor Owen, Parliamentary Correspondent

An effort to clear Britain's streets of beggars was urged by Mr John Major yesterday.

The prime minister called on the public to be 'rigorous' in reporting beggars to the police. He pointed out that they could be fined up to £1,000 and jailed for up to three years if they resorted to violence.

Mr Major's blunt condemnation of the increasing number of vagrants who regularly beg in London and other city centres was fiercely attacked by political opponents and officials of leading charities.

Mr John Battle, shadow housing minister, said the government should tackle the real problems of poverty and homelessness.

Withdrawals of benefits for people aged 16 and 17 had forced many young people on to the streets - and the benefits should be reinstated, he said.

Mr Charles Kennedy, president of the Liberal Democrats, denounced the prime minister's attack on the homeless as 'an absolute outrage'.

Mr Nick Hardwick, director of Centrepoint, the young people's charity, said fining young beggars was daft.

'They simply have to beg to raise the money to pay it off again,' he said.

'What offends people is not the beggars themselves, but that in one of the wealthiest countries in the world so many young people and others who cannot look after themselves should be forced to beg.'

However, Mr Peter Bottomley, Conservative MP for Eltham, said he had encountered a man begging for food who had difficulty walking because his pockets were 'full of cash'.

Mr Bottomley said: 'I brought him a hamburger, a Coke and chips. But he had more money on him than I did.

In an interview with the Bristol Evening Post, the prime minister insisted that there could be no justification for people to be 'out on the street'.

Beggars were an eyesore and could drive tourists and shoppers away from cities. They caused offence to many and their activities were particularly damaging to areas dependent on tourism.

Mr Major maintained that the social security system made begging unnecessary, and called on those responsible not to shrink from enforcing the rigorous penalties that were available.

Asked if he thought people should report beggars to the police, the prime minister replied: 'Yes certainly, most certainly.'